TRANSFORMED *by* TRAGEDY

A ROSE OF REDEMPTION

Carmyn Sparks

Carpenter's Son Publishing

Transformed by Tragedy: A Rose of Redemption

©2013 by Carmyn Sparks

Published by Carpenter's Son Publishing, Franklin, Tennessee

Published in association with Larry Carpenter of Christian Book Services, LLC
www.christianbookservices.com

Cover and Interior Design by Suzanne Lawing

Editing by Robert Irvin

Printed in the United States of America

978-1-940262-01-7

WHAT PEOPLE ARE SAYING
ABOUT THIS BOOK

TRANSFORMED BY TRAGEDY is a gripping saga exposing secret sins of a powerful West Texas family. Many were envious of Carmyn's seemingly privileged life as a wealthy society debutante but underneath the ball gowns and jewels there was a tormented little girl. This beautifully written tragedy is sometimes shockingly painful to read but ultimately with the intervention of a loving Savior through the prayers of an unlikely heroine there is victory and healing. Thanks to Carmyn's bravery and boldness, and God's mercy and grace, countless other victims will be transformed by this book.

 —**Ron Hall**, author of New York Times best seller *SAME KIND OF DIFFERENT AS ME.*

"It is a wonderful blessing when we can recognize the hand of God throughout the journey of our life. Carmyn Sparks invites us into the story of her life and shows us glimpses of God's love and comfort at every turn. Through the pain and difficulties, as well as the joyful moments, we are reminded of God's presence and strength. *Transformed by Tragedy* offers a framework for each of us to recognize God's redemptive work in the midst of our struggles."

 —**Karol Ladd**, author of *Positive Life Principles for Women*

Everyone has a past. Much of, if not most of who we are today and who we may become, is linked to what has happened to us in the past. For far too many, those events have been deeply hurtful standing in the way of the present and the yet-to-be. Carmyn has dared to confront full-on the painful past thus freeing herself from its damaging effects. This is a book about the transformative power of asking for God's help and then trusting Him to walk through the present and the unknown future in the strength of His freeing, forgiving, merciful and loving care. You will be blessed and helped as you read this honest and touching memoir.

    —**Helen K. Hosier**, biographer and author of *100 Christian Women Who Changed the 20th Century*

FOREWORD

Carmyn's spell-binding story illustrates the compelling truth that if you struggle with the effects of verbal, or emotional, or physical or sexual abuse, you can truly find transformational healing from God through Jesus.

Interestingly, we respond to things according to the meanings those things have for us. So we respond to events by asking ourselves: "What does this mean?" Sometimes, we are smart enough to ask: "What else could this mean?" Certainly, our lives would be happier, if we asked: "What would I like this to mean?"

Unfortunately, children ask themselves only: "What does this mean?" And often: "What does this mean about me?" So if abuse happened, the meanings given to the event and to themselves, would usually be negative meanings.

Unfortunately, children form meanings and then form meanings about those meanings. That often means that an abused child usually takes the fact of being abused and makes it mean: "People are dangerous, I am a victim, I am worthless, I'll never amount to anything, I am a failure in life, I am unloved, I am unlovable, I deserve bad things, something's wrong with me, I am a loser, etc." And there are people who encourage abused people to hold on to those meanings--meanings which the child gave in ignorance.

Fortunately, healing comes from changing negative meanings into positive ones. The first change needs to be that the abuse didn't mean anything negative about the child, but it meant many negative things about the abuser. Then a transformational moment comes when the adult accepts the truth that whatever happened in the past is truly past, and Jesus is asking: "What do you want your future to be?"

This book fascinatingly shows what happens when the adult answers that last question.

Dr. Kembleton Wiggins
Doctor of Education
Doctor of Pastoral Counseling
Certified Life Coach.

CONTENTS

Carmyn and Rosetta 1971 at Hal and Carmyn's Wedding

PROLOGUE: ROSETTA'S LEGACY

On June 15, 2010 which was the day before my sixty-first birthday, Rosetta's niece, Linda, called around 2 PM. She was sobbing so hard that I couldn't understand her. After a few seconds she finally collected herself and said, "Rosetta is gone." We both wept and said we'd talk again later when we were more composed.

Finally, thirteen days later, on June 28, Rosetta's body was driven from Beaumont, Texas to Fort Worth, Texas in a white hearse. Her funeral service was held at the Lake Como Church of Christ. My family sat with Rosetta's family, and I gave a tribute to her life.

On the day of the funeral service I was the first family member to arrive at the church; walked into the sanctuary alone to view Rosetta's body. Slowly approaching the open casket, I held my breath. I was afraid to see sweet Rosetta's lifeless body in the coffin.

But when I looked at the lining in the top of her casket, I noticed there was one pink rose embroidered in the fabric. What a fitting tribute to Rosetta's life. Her family had chosen the rose emblem to honor her memory. Precisely fifty-seven years before, on an early June morning in 1953, Rosetta had appeared in my life. June is my birthday month, and roses are my birth flower. I drew a deep breath as a surge of emotions flooded my heart. It was like time stood still for a brief moment, and memory-filled pictures flashed through my mind of our extraordinary journey together—a black woman and a white child. With loving care Rosetta taught me so much, like how to tie my shoes and brush my hair—so many of the practical tasks in life. But more importantly, she was the answer to my childhood prayers as she taught me how to live in the midst of the many tragic events unfolding in my young life. The blessed reality of God's purpose for Rosetta being in my life seemed to be unveiled before me as I stood alongside the casket holding her body. She was indeed like a rose. The sweet fragrance of her life has left behind an everlasting fragrance of blessings, lingering on long after the last petal has fallen from the flower.

Rosetta's niece, Linda, had asked me to give the eulogy at Rosetta's service. Now I knew just the words I would use to describe her kind and wise influence in shaping my life.

TRIBUTE TO MAMA ROSE

The funeral service began with prayers, the reading of some of Rosetta's favorite Scriptures, and one of her favorite hymns, "Steal Away to Jesus," by Wallace Willis. I was then asked to come forward, and as I walked to the podium, I looked out and saw my husband, three daughters with their husbands, and six grandchildren sitting with Rosetta's family, and also her church family. The slight nervousness I was feeling left me. There wasn't any reason to feel nervous, for I was at home with those who loved and respected Rosetta. Her church family and friends embraced me as Rosetta's "white" child. This was where I was meant to be. And so, that June day, I spoke these words from my heart that was overflowing with joy and peace because of Mama Rose.

"One of the most powerful contributions a human being can make is to have a positive impact in a child's life.

"Occasionally, a particular moment permanently alters us and may remain a beacon throughout our lives, serving to prompt a certain quality in our own lives, such as nurturing love and kindness. For me, I was fortunate to have such a precious gift arise in my life . . .

"In June 1953, when I was only four years old and Rosetta thirty-six, she came into my life. Little did I know what a priceless influence Rosetta Williams would contribute over the course of her life to mine.

"If ever a person came to earth and did what God had sent them to do, it was Rosetta.

"As a child, I was desperate for a connection to a loving presence.

"In a childhood that was mostly unhappy, Rosetta shines brightly as the protective angel that God sent to be the continual voice of acceptance and approval.

"In my hard times, she was an ally when I had no other, and in her presence I experienced unfailing love. She was my teacher, and

she taught a love that endures regardless of circumstances.

"As a reliable and nurturing caregiver, Rosetta provided structure and a routine. Days in the kitchen snapping peas or kneading dough were the simple activities that slowed the unstable pace of life for me and marked significantly the passages of time Rosetta and I shared together, which served to forge a deep bond between us.

"These days I hear her voice in many directions of my life . . . the wisdom and trust of God alone to forgive. She instilled in me character qualities seldom seen in my own family.

"Rosetta taught me to pick myself up and be strong, to forge ahead in spite of circumstances, the unfairness of life, the cruelty of injustice and the emotional pain of rejection.

"Throughout the times Rosetta and I shared, just the two of us, our races were separated by the limitations society placed upon us. But we experienced what few this side of Heaven get to know, the blessed truth of equality that has no barriers of race, culture, or status. We were each helping the other to find the way. Our hands, one dark and one white, clasped tightly, one to protect and the other to trust.

"For years after I was no longer under Rosetta's direct care, her strong and caring hands continued to work through mine as I cooked, cleaned, and prayed. Her comforting arms and gentle heart showed me the way to love and care for my own family. Rosetta's nurturing care was the foundation for the motherly love I was later able to give my own children.

"Her unspoken guidance has stayed with me and is implanted deep within my soul. Her life example has been the root of my spiritual longing, as her trust and faith in God pointed the way to a deeper spiritual experience for me.

"From knowing—but more importantly experiencing—Rosetta's love, I learned that once the heart has been pierced by love, there can be no turning back nor any denial of this truth, as the heart will search until it finds its rest in God alone.

"Her care served as a balm for the mistreatment and loneliness I experienced as a child, and she became the healer of my* *wounded soul, as her prayers were the instrument that led me to our Savior, Jesus Christ.*

"Rosetta was my first Rose, as I affectionately called her Mama Rose. Through her prayers and love I have been blessed with my own rose garden, my precious husband, children, and adoring grandchildren, all of whom serve and proclaim Jesus Christ as Lord.

"My last day with her was magic . . . because we both knew it would be our last. Our hearts ached and our eyes spilled over with tears. How could we say good-bye?

"But it was time, and both of us knew the hard business of letting go had reached its end—saying good-bye was hard.

"But now my heart rejoices in the hope she gave me that is stronger than sorrow and grief.

"Her sweet memory is a source of life and inspiration to all who hold her dear, and the legacy she leaves will continue to bless each with her strong faith and enduring love.

"Good-bye, my sweet Mama Rose. Good-bye, until we are together again."

The congregation stood and applauded as many wept. I knew this was not for me, and not even for Rosetta, but for the awesome power of God to impart love and acceptance through one ordinary person to another.

As I took my place on the front pew and sat down, my mind and thoughts called to remembrance the words of the poet Soren Kierkegaard, who wrote: "Life can only be understood backwards, but it must be lived forwards."

Looking back, it was clear now why Carmyn was my chosen name—and especially the Y in my name. This book tells the story of the "why" of the Y in my name!

CHAPTER 1

THE "Y" OF CARMYN

*In every life there is a beginning, but thankfully, beginnings
do not necessarily foretell the end.*

Anxiously anticipating my birth, Father nervously paced in the waiting room of the maternity ward. Occasionally he retreated outside to smoke a cigarette from his three-packs-a-day Lucky Strike habit which, he maintained, were "calming." The year was 1949 and cigarettes had not yet been banned in public places, but as funny as it now seems, smoking was forbidden around his mother even at his age of twenty-eight.

His mother, my paternal grandmother, had fire-engine red hair that matched her quick-trigger temper. Those who feared her most secretly referred to her as Big Red. In the corner of the waiting room, Big Red sat solemnly next to my grandfather while he twiddled his thumbs on a protruding belly, which somewhat resembled that of the expectant mother. Big Red's presence alone commanded authority, so no one dared question the prohibition against smoking in her presence, not even her son nor her husband.

I was my parents' second born, their firstborn having been a male heir destined to carry on the family name to succeeding generations. My two-year-old brother was blond and hazel-eyed and, of course, was the chosen one who captured the heart of the family. Because he was, indeed, the designated male heir, Big Red was especially taken with him. As the years passed he became the favored one of my grandparents. Big Red eventually assumed most of his upbringing.

My father was uneasy about his second child's birth; there were unanswered questions about the forthcoming child that concerned him and also his parents, which was why their presence at the hospital was deemed necessary. Whatever their fears may have been at the time, the three of them were apparently anxious about the second born child waiting to be bestowed upon their family.

Name Assignment

If the baby turned out to be a girl, the name assignment had already been decided. Her name would be Constance, and they would call her Connie. She would not be given a middle name or initial because Father wanted his daughter to carry her maiden name all through her life, even following marriage.

As the nurse carried the newborn through the delivery room doors, gasps must have come from all three. I looked like a little Hispanic baby with thick black hair, brown eyes, and an olive complexion. "You have a little girl," the nurse delightedly exclaimed. Father beamed with pride, as his new daughter bore a natural resemblance to him. He announced, "This is my daughter," then received me from the nurse, held me up, and said, "Her name is C...A...R...M...Y...N. Carmyn with a 'Y.'"

My grandparents were surprised and a bit disappointed that they had just witnessed the entry of a new granddaughter. This was because males in our family were esteemed more highly than females, at least according to the paternal side of the family. And . . . the name—where did Father get his choice of a name for me? Everyone just assumed it was because he loved operas and arrived at that name from the Spanish gypsy in the opera *Carmen*.

THE "Y" IN WHY?

Actually, no one knows why or how Father chose that name and especially the Y in my name. This unusual spelling causes common mispronunciations, as well as misspelling, even to this day. My grandfather always knew there was a Y in my name somewhere, but in spelling it, he was never able to put it in the same place; hence, his diverse spellings of my name as Carymn, Camryn and Carmny.

Looking back, I believe that this Y in my name was the beginning of my feeling much like a misplaced "why" in life. That lack of identity in early childhood foreshadowed, unbeknownst to me, significant difficulties and troubles ahead.

On the eventful day of my birth, my mother and I became separated, both literally and figuratively. This proved to be symbolic in that she either was unable—or chose not to be—a nurturing mother. Nursing her second born was most assuredly not appealing to Mother—so she didn't. Since Mother lived mostly out of her own need for love, she had not the maternal instinct or inclination to provide motherly care to her newborn daughter. So began, both symbolically and actually, the conflictual struggles between Mother and me. As time would bear out, these struggles would continue and intensify from that time on.

FORT WORTH IN THE 1950S

Among Fort Worth's social elite in the 1950's baby nurses were the norm. A Ms. Rainwater was employed to care for me during my first year of life. She took charge over all my physical needs, fed and bathed me, and changed my diapers. To this day, I have no idea who Ms. Rainwater was, and I only know of her because her name is written in my baby book. Whether she sang me a lullaby, talked soothingly, or prayed gently to my yearning soul, I know not.

After Ms. Rainwater left, my caretakers were domestics hired by Father. Father made sure his household ran efficiently, especially since he worked from dawn to dusk. During the 1950s most wealthy families, particularly in the Southwest, relied on hired help to do all the gritty and necessary tasks of housework. These societal wives were usually kept busy with outside community work, days playing bridge at the Club, shopping, or being away on trips. However, in our case, Mother's alcoholism made her unable to effectively function without daily assistance. In our household the domestic help was responsible to oversee not only the daily chores of our home, but the care of the baby and any other children as well. As time went by, I felt more at home with and dependent on our help, rather than with my own family members.

From early childhood I longed for, but was deprived of, the nurturing love of a caring mother. That longing of mine became a quest for unfailing love which I searched for throughout my formative years, teens, and the early years of young adulthood, attempting to fill an emptiness of soul. This was just the beginning of my pursuit of the many "whys" in life to come in the years that lay ahead.

For someone like me, this was not a very promising beginning.

CHAPTER 2

PARENT-GRANDPARENT ISSUES

This is the way life was for me when I was very young.

The relationship between Mother and Big Red, my paternal grand-mother, was intriguing but difficult, and sometimes outright hostile. Even more interesting was the mysterious relational triangle among Father, Mother, and Big Red. I've never understood the power that Big Red held over my parents, but I do know that money, with its alluring privileges, was one of the major contributing factors in the control dynamic omnipresent throughout the years.

This grandmother was a powerful and domineering matriarch, and both my parents were submissive and placating to her presumptive position of authority. Soon after their wedding, my parents moved into my paternal grandparents' large Spanish-style mansion in an en-clave for the wealthy elite. They lived with my father's parents until after I was born some three years later.

MOTHER'S ULTIMATUM

A year after I gained entrance into this world, Mother gave Father an ultimatum for them to move out of his parents' home. Somewhat surprisingly, he managed to act against Big Red's preferences and bought Mother a home of their own. While Big Red had never been fond of Mother, this ultimatum created an even deeper split, adding to the ever-increasing animosity between them. This shared family feud lasted until the day of Big Red's death in 1983.

HOUSES

Houses are how I recall the time frames of my childhood. When I was two years old, one night in the big Spanish house, I was awakened by a loud and explosive "bang" noise. Sitting up in bed, I was frightened by this sound. I'd never heard that sound before and was far too young to understand what was going on. Now I can only imagine what it must have been like. There it went again, followed by slamming and yelling, feet pounding, and angry voices. "I'm going to kill you, you so-and-so," a familiar voice raged.

Frantically, I attempted to hide and put my head under the pillow and trembled with fear. Right away my four-year-old brother was there and put his arms around me and whispered, "It's going to be OK." Then there was another explosive bang and another angry yell. Then nothing. An eerie quiet followed, which only compounded our fear of what might happen next.

Brother and I just sat there on the bed, our huddled shadows outlined on the wall from an outside light source coming through the window shades. I was shaking and trying not to cry, but then he said, "Look." And Brother began making shadow figures on the wall with his hands. He made those shadow figures come alive and dance on the wall. At the same time, he made silly little noises, pretending to be a bunny, an alligator, or a bird; it mesmerized me and took my mind off my fears. I think it did him, too.

I don't know how long Brother entertained me, but finally feeling safe and somewhat secure, I must have fallen asleep, because that's all I remember of that night. It must have been a very traumatic experience for both of us in order for me, as a two-year-old, to have remembered it these many years later. It wouldn't be until a half-century later, when I asked Brother, that I learned the complete story about this incident. He said, "Oh yeah, that was the night our grandmother chased grand-dad with a gun and shot him in the foot." This incident of household violence at the hands of Big Red did not bode well for me and failed to prepare me for those yet to come. This was the way life continued throughout my early childhood.

THE LITTLE WHITE HOUSE

When I was three years old, I remember the precious little white house that was our first home. It was a comparatively small brick house with a glassed-in back porch. Our new house was barely more than 1,500 square feet, and the back porch had been turned into my bedroom. There were pretty white eyelet curtains on the windows, and my daybed was beneath one of the side windows.

At night the street light flickered softly through the tiny holes in those curtains, dimly illuminating little dots of light on the wall opposite my bed. Those dots of soft light became my friends to which I gave names: White Dot, Little White Dot, Big White Dot, and so on. I watched them dance playfully on windy nights, or when it was calm weather I sometimes stared at their stillness and felt strangely alone.

As a placating token to his mother, Father provided her gratuitous entrance to our new home and implicit permission to intrude by giving Big Red a key. Apparently this was because my parents were often not at home and out of town quite a lot. Mother repeatedly demanded that Father keep Big Red out of their marital and family matters, but as usual, Father was unable to break loose from the invisible umbilical cord still attached, relationally speaking. As a consequence, the dominant control over our family matters by Big Red relentlessly continued. Big Red would indirectly oversee our household, from both near and far, because Father was in the dysfunctional mode of mostly trying to please his parents instead of his wife. The grandparents' long sought—but rarely attained—approval was a driving force in his submissive behavior. Father's latent inability and unwillingness to grasp the essence of his role as husband in the marital relationship continued. This fundamentally divisive issue of not being able to fulfill the proper role of a husband was a bitter source of contention throughout my parents' marriage.

CHAPTER 3

BALL OF LIGHT

The Light was not just a way out of the darkness,
but the way through it.

I don't know the name of the nice lady who took care of me in my pre-kindergarten days, but as was always the case, Big Red regularly showed up at our new home ranting and raving about one thing or another. She even exercised enough control to command one babysitter to leave. As was her inexplicable wont, Big Red would occasionally take me with her to the big Spanish House. There she resided with Grandfather and, usually, Brother. However, on one particularly cold night that was not the case.

THE LOCK-IN

In our kitchen at home, I'd been sitting on the counter eating cookies with the babysitter when Big Red arrived. As always, it was her custom to use a personal house key to enter our home unannounced.

Big Red fussed about something and then told me to get in bed and go to sleep. Quickly I ran to my room and then heard her yell at the babysitter. For whatever reason, Big Red always seemed to be mad or angry about something. She was hard to please and I never felt liked or enjoyed by her. In fact, all outward indications were that she hated me. I remember Big Red often saying that they—which I presumed to be my family—did not want (or like) little girls.

Because the side of my back porch bedroom facing the outside was lined with windows, it was easily the coldest room in our home when winter settled in. On this particular night, Big Red turned up the fire in the gas heater situated in one corner of my room. Being just three at the time, I had no idea what upset her, but she stormed out of my room and slammed the door shut. Then I heard the door lock click. She had locked my bedroom door from the other side. I ran to the door and grabbed the handle to open it, but it wouldn't budge. A sensation of fright in the pit of my stomach came over me. I screamed, begging for someone to come and open the door. I was really scared, because usually the bedroom door would be left open for me. But it was not to be left unlocked this foreboding night.

I sat next to the door for what seemed like an eternity, but no one came in response to my pleading cries. I was locked in, trapped in my own bedroom. I was alone with the tiny white dots of light dancing on the wall. A sense of abandonment and despair overwhelmed me. Forced to surrender any futile attempts or hope of escape, I fell upon my bed a sad and disheartened little girl. My cries failed to bring any aid for my rescue.

It seemed like either my parents, or Big Red, or both from time to time, were in a constant mode of pulling and yanking on me like a rag doll. Depending on who happened to be in charge at the time, I was either slapped, rudely shaken, spat on, or pinched and yelled at. But what hurt more than anything were the cruel words that I wasn't wanted and was nothing but trouble. These painful shards ripped like cut glass at my soul's frail edges. Feelings of being unwanted, unloved, and intensely disliked cut through my child's heart like a cold, steel knife.

THE GAS HEATER

Blue, orange, and gold luminous lights flickered in the dark from the flames from the gas heater in the corner of my bedroom, slowly attracting my attention. This may have been the beginning of my embedded feelings of deep unworthiness. Feeling forgotten and forsaken, I became drowsy from the overpowering heat. I drifted off into a light sleep. Sleep was short, and I awoke with my nightgown soaked with perspiration. As the heat continued to increase in my oxygen-starved room, it began to feel like the inside of an oven. Listless, I slipped out of the bed and crawled to the door, reaching up once more, grabbing the doorknob. The handle was so hot; my small fingers slipped around it in a futile attempt to open the door.

Before being made into a bedroom, the back porch door had originally been a door to the outside of the house. That's why the door lock was on the wrong side of that door. So now there wasn't any way for me to unlock the door from the inside. In quiet desperation and fear for my life, I began and continued to knock repeatedly on the door. My knuckles on both hands were now so tender that I gave up and sat down.

The red brick floor of my room, usually cool to my bare legs, was extremely hot. As I could bear no more, from the depths of this unremitting torment, I cried out and begged God, or anyone, "Please help me!"

THE WHITE LIGHT

Hot air filled the bedroom oppressively and made it hard for me to breathe. I felt sleep closing in again, but then a bright white light appeared, filling a dark corner of my room with its luminous glow. In the center of this white light, amber gold colors faded into pure, clear, and clean rays filled with tiny glitters of luminescent white dots.

I saw no one and heard nothing, but intuitively knew I was not alone. This bright glittering circle of light slowly moved toward me. Amazingly, I no longer felt afraid, but my eyes were heavy and I struggled to keep them open. I gradually became aware that the white light was moving even closer. The warmth of a quiet peace and a sense of safety and well-being flooded my body. Then I lost consciousness.

THE GREAT RESCUE

This event was reapeatedly told to me through the years by Mother. Mother called it *"the just-in-time great rescue."* She said, "Just by chance, Father and I returned home two hours earlier than expected."

Albeit, drunk, Father noticed my bedroom door was closed. Since Father knew if I awakened to find my door closed, my screams for help might disturb him, he shrewdly opened my door to prevent an interruption to his sleep.

As he opened the door, hot air suddenly blasted his face. He stumbled backwards and quickly noticed me lying on the floor. He muttered, "Oh for God's sake," as he picked me up and placed me in bed. Somewhat annoyed, he turned off the gas heater and opened a window for the room to ventilate.

Big Red casually remarked, "The room was cold. I closed the door to let it warm up the room."

Once again, no one dared to question Big Red's behavior.

So this was the great rescue that Father was always given credit for saving me from a more serious fate that cold night.

YES, FOR GOD'S SAKE

Truly, for God's sake, my life was spared but in reality, not by Father. A radiant Light appeared as a magnificent spirit. It came to see me through the troubling darkness and oppressive heat. This Light was not just a way out of the darkness, but through the present, and unbeknown to me, was sent to see me through the future.

Death's bid in this instance would come near, but would not triumph. I live now to bear witness to the Light. And the Light has become my friend for life. This was the beginning of several times in later years when the beautiful and glorious Light appeared in my life. It would be years later before the Light revealed Himself. Moving forward in life it was unclear *who* was the Light, but at the right time, in the right way, and in the right order, years later, would I fully grasp what had happened this dark night of my soul, and know that the Light was the strength that carried me throughout the traumatic years ahead.

CHAPTER 4

THE BEAUTIFUL THIN LADY AND HER VARIABLE MOODS

The few visits I had with her were rarely the same.

When Brother was six and I was four, my parents moved into a new, larger house. Their new abode was located in a new housing subdivision, and it was large compared to our former house. Thankfully, my bedroom was far from my parents, but Brother's room was right down the hallway. I was always glad when he was home because I didn't feel nearly as isolated and alone.

My bedroom was cold and rarely felt warm. Because I was usually fearful and afraid, even Brother's presence nearby didn't diminish my fears. There were times we created some intermittent moments of fun and laughter together. While that helped, it didn't serve to fully lessen my fear-filled daily life.

PARENTS' PROBLEMS

Our parents regularly had gatherings of loud and raucous friends over to our house for drinks and conversation at night. From my bed-room, I could hear their cocktail glasses clinking with ice; the adults reeked with alcohol smells and I saw their insensate, intoxicated be-havior with its unpleasant side effects. Sounds of boisterous and un-ruly adults, imbibing cocktails without restraint, filled our home on these occasions.

At age thirty-two, Father wore heavy, black-rimmed glasses, and he had coal black hair, which was slicked straight back with Vitalis hair oil. Resembling Al Capone, he would parade me through the festive sunroom filled with lively strangers. Father's bar was replete with every variety of alcoholic beverages known to man. The air was heavy with clouds of cigarette smoke and the stench of bourbon and scotch permeated the sun-room and its occupants. The ladies wore fancy cocktail dresses, fashionable for the 1950s, and sparkled with their gaudy diamond rings, necklaces, and other colorful jewelry. The men usually wore dark suits with ties undone, and the collars of their white business shirts unbuttoned. All in attendance at these societal get-togethers held burning cigarettes in their manicured fingers (the men's fingers, too).

I felt awkward and like a puppet on display, as it was my appointed duty to tell all present goodnight at about 8 pm. Most of the guests ap-peared to be talking in slow motion and would slur their words. Father would say, "Give 'Aunt Nancy' a kiss goodnight." And so, around the room, I was paraded to give goodnight kisses to these smelly strangers whom, for some reason, I was to call "Aunt and Uncle."

SOME FUN TIMES

On some occasions Brother communicated to Father through the maid that the noise from the party room was too loud for us to sleep. Father gladly gave his permission for us to be taken to the one room normally forbidden, except on very special occasions, that being our parents' bedroom. This is where we had some fun times while they partied, oblivious to us children while they reveled on throughout the night.

I loved entering into their large, high-ceilinged bedroom. It was beautiful and ornate with gold trim filigree and different shades of green. There were so many beautiful things to look at that I longed to touch and explore, but this was prohibited. Most pretty things in the house were off limits to me and were considered untouchable. I didn't think we lived in a museum, but it sure reminded me of one during the day. The formal living, sun, and music rooms were devoid of people during the day, but were always perfect in appearance, neat and cold.

Although there were not any "Do Not Touch" signs, each room had an ostentatious air that said it all. My mother, "The Beautiful Thin Lady," liked everything in her house to appear perfect (including me). The furnishings were far too showy for the likes of young children. There were gilded, gold-trim waste baskets all around our house, but there was never any trash in them. Once, while going through the living room, I threw a Kleenex in one of the trash baskets. "No, no, no! Don't throw that in there!" Those were the words spoken by Mother when she suddenly showed up at the most inopportune moments.

FURNITURE ARRANGEMENTS

On one side of my parents' bedroom was a chair with a bench seat so long you could lie down on it. The tables were full of tiny cut glass or crystal figurines and flowery cloisonné boxes of mostly oriental décor. Ivory Chinese men and women, mean-faced Japanese Foo dogs (the tradition of these dogs is to scare off evil spirits, but it sure didn't help at our house!), and various colors of Imari jars and vases filled almost every nook and cranny in Mother's house. Fresh flowers were arranged in tall oriental vases, and long chartreuse and hunter green print drapes hung on floor-to-ceiling windows, keeping the room dark, unless the floor length curtains were opened or the lights turned on.

The only other place where I might see The Beautiful Thin Lady, who mostly lived in this bedroom, was at her dressing room table with the three mirrors surrounding it. This table was particularly elegant and exquisitely decorated. The most beautiful bottles of various bright colors and hues lined her dressing table. Tiny round white light bulbs outlined the mirrors, while silver brushes, colored pencils, and all sorts of lipsticks adorned the mirrored tabletop. Three mirrors encased the dressing table, one in front and one on each side. I loved to stand on her vanity stool as I watched the movement of my hands and legs in the three mirrors. It was so cool! The triple mirrors reflecting into each other made it look like my image went on forever.

Mother's closet went on forever too. I could get lost in there behind the silky, long satin dresses and furs. The dressing room table jewelry boxes were filled to the brim with assorted jewelry that sparkled and glistened, and she even had little bell earrings that chimed. Buried beneath the clothes were books full of naked people. Something disturbed me about these books, so I only opened one of them once.

MOTHER AND HER VARIABLE MOODS

On the few occasions I was allowed to see The Beautiful Thin Lady in her bedroom, she usually was seated in front of the dressing table mirror. She was a smoker too, and she was rarely without a lit cigarette perched on the edge of one of the many ornate ashtrays. Her eyes would catch mine, and she would sometimes motion me to come forward with an inviting "Darling." She held her cheek out for me to give her a kiss.

But other times she would cry or whimper softly. Sometimes she would speak incoherently, and sometimes she would just yell "Get out!" The few visits to her bedroom I had with her were rarely the same.

I usually saw the bed tray being taken to her by the kitchen maid in the morning and might be lucky to see her in the afternoon, or possibly at dinner, but she didn't eat much.

WONDERFUL ESCAPES

The bed in our parents' bedroom was the largest I'd ever seen and had more pillows than I could count. Close by the bed was a gorgeous mahogany desk, and on its desktop were lots of pencils and pens in a pretty pink box with pink minuet roses painted on top. There was even a pen with a feather on it and another pink box with stamps in it. One night Brother and I carefully opened a drawer and found several wooden pencils, one with a purple football on the end. Brother broke the wooden football off and taught me how to play knuckle football.

Our fingers were the players running to score. I had a really hard time trying to kick the ball with my tiny fingers. But when Brother flicked the ball, it would fly. Immediately, we started another game of seeing how far he could make the little football go. It was a rare event full of fun and laughter. Finally, I was too tired to play anymore, so I crawled up on the bed and lay my head down on one of the pretty satin pillows. Soon I was fast asleep.

I was never allowed to wake up the next morning in The Beautiful Thin Lady's bedroom. The nice colored lady who dressed me always woke me in the mornings, and somehow I had miraculously ended up back in my bedroom in my own bed. Another colored lady took care of Brother, so we seldom saw each other during the day; most of the time it seemed like he was with Big Red, either at her home or at the Ranch. I only know that, from the ages of two to twelve, we seldom saw each other.

Even so, these were some welcomed times of fun and laughter when Brother and I played together. They were fantasy-world excursions from the usual dreadful days and awful nighttimes. Those few episodes of normal childhood activities enabled me to experience brief respites from the sad reality of the present.

CHAPTER 5

SHADOWS AND SNAKES

My worst nightmares . . . were some of the most
awful experiences of my life. I don't know why I was told
to fear rattlesnakes during the day, because in my life,
they came out mostly at night.

My worst nightmares came at night, naturally. But they were not dreams; they were some of the most awful experiences of my life. It began one night after all had gone to bed when, strangely, The Shadow appeared and entered my bedroom for the first time. I didn't want to believe The Shadow was my father, so I pretended it was a bad man. The bad man's figure created a silhouette in the dim light as he entered the room. It cast a dark shadow against the hall wall. When my bedroom door was closed, the light from the hall was shut out. Now there was nothing but the blackness in my room and the presence of the bad man.

As he approached my bed, I closed my eyes and prayed for The Shadow to leave. The smell of stale cigarette smoke and the awful smell of what I now know to be Scotch whiskey overcame me. And I felt the heavy pressure of his weight bearing down on my face and body. Feeling like I might stop breathing, I was transported to the ceiling in weightlessness, but then was surrounded by the warmth of my friend, The Light. Then finally, The Shadow lifted off of me and The Shadow disappeared. It was real and yet not real, but the reality of the ordeal would jar my body, and many times from then on, after The Shadow disappeared, I would throw up.

Brother and I never said anything about The Shadow, but I knew intuitively he couldn't make The Shadow disappear. We both knew there was nothing within a child's power that could be done about the abusive adults in our lives.

FRIGHTFUL NIGHTS

Many nights after that, I was so scared to stay in my room that I took my pillow and hid behind a chair in the living room to sleep. Sometimes I slept on the floor in front of the room where I was not allowed to enter. When I cried and begged not to be put back in my bedroom, I was made to return.

Crying and begging proved to be a huge mistake.

DRILL SERGEANT

One hot summer morning in 1953, before the sun had risen, The Man in Black-Rimmed Glasses, my father, placed me in his car for an eight-hour-long drive to south Texas. It wasn't until early nightfall that we reached our destination, a ranch house in a cactus-filled sprawling ranch setting. Once off the highway, he drove us on a graveled dirt road for several miles until we finally made it to the only house in sight. I'd never seen so much cacti and barren grassless earth. Once there I was left with a tall, masculine woman and a large man, her husband and my "uncle." She was known to be a "drill-sergeant" with an emphasis on curt discipline. I learned quickly to do whatever she said, when she said it to do it, and to do it her way. If not, I suffered the rapid consequence of being whipped across the back of my legs with her leather belt.

This Drill Sergeant, my mother's older sister, was my childless aunt. They had no children, nor intended to have any, not ever. But paradoxically, she was confident that she could do a better job of obedience training than my mother. I was made her "discipline" project at the early age of four years old.

PONY INCIDENT

My babysitter that summer turned out to be a pony, and I was deposited on the pony and told not to get off because of all the rattlesnakes around the area. "Don't get off this pony," the Drill Sergeant sternly commanded me.

While I had thought it hot during summers in Fort Worth, this was the hottest place I'd ever been. The pony and I must have gone round and round in circles in the horse pen for hours. Finally, the poor pony got so tired and hot that he just lay down on the ground. Then I pulled on the reins and finally got the worn-out pony back up on his feet. Since I was so small, I was unable to make it back up on the saddle. So, out of frustration and fear of the rattlesnakes, I fearfully began to walk the pony back to the ranch house a hundred yards or so away.

My act of misread disobedience was met with rage by the Drill Sergeant. "I told you not to get off that horse!" . . . but before I could reply, her belt was blistering my legs. Through streaming tears I said, "But the pony lay down."

While there was no apology for the wrongful whipping, her belly laughter could be heard for miles. This purposeless story would be told over and over again by The Drill Sergeant (and my mother), lasting until I reached adulthood. Being the recipient of the unjust whipping, it certainly didn't seem funny to me at the time, nor afterward.

ANOTHER NIGHT VISITOR

My resistance to this harsh adult supervision also manifested itself at night at this ranch. I hated sleeping by myself, because for some reason The Shadow, which came alive at my house in Fort Worth, also came alive down in South Texas. The Drill Sergeant's husband, my uncle, would come into my bedroom at his ranch during the late night. I don't know why I was told to fear rattlesnakes during the day, because in my life, they came out mostly at night.

One particular night I begged The Drill Sergeant not to leave me in my assigned bedroom alone. Hysterical, I held onto her and cried uncontrollably. The gripping cloak of fear was overwhelming, until finally I threw up all over the floor. The Drill Sergeant was furious and told me I'd done that on purpose. I was given a spoon and bucket and told to clean up my own vomit.

After the mess was cleaned up and the door closed, it was only a matter of time before a dark shadow appeared and crawled into my bed. My uncle was here again, just as I feared. As Lamont Cranston once said, "Who knows what evil lurks in the hearts of men? The Shadow knows!" (The quote is from a famous 1930s radio program series named *The Shadow*.) Only, in my case, the evil manifested itself in two male adults, and I had no viable means of escape, nor any effective means of appeal.

HOME AGAIN, FINALLY

After six long weeks of unbridled fury visited upon me in south Texas, I finally left that miserable ranch and was brought home. The Drill Sergeant announced proudly to my parents that I'd finally learned how to sleep in a room by myself. But, by the end of my first night home, I was driven back by well-founded fears to the familiar hiding place behind the chair in the living room.

It would be a year before I returned to the south Texas desert. And upon hearing I must go again, I reported to The Beautiful Thin Lady that my Uncle would come into the room and put his hands on me. She merely laughed and replied, "Oh, he does that to everyone." I learned later, at age twenty, that he had been found on several occasions beneath the bed of my Aunt's friends, who visited them at their ranch from time to time. Her casual remark only confused my understanding of the event, *Didn't anyone find his behavior strange?*

I was afraid and ashamed to tell anyone about the shadows and snakes that kept coming alive during the nights, as I feared their ridicule—"You're just imagining things"—and their flat nonresponse. Especially since the lack of motherly care and protection in my life involved even other things that didn't seen to matter to The Beautiful Thin Lady. However, I was truly ashamed to share these unthinkable secrets with anyone else, especially since my own Mother laughed them off. So I kept silent. Naturally, I was always fearful of the shadows and snakes that appeared during dark nights, both at home and in South Texas. That ongoing saga of misery and shame occurring repeatedly in my childhood was to continue for a very long time.

I learned from all of this that no matter who was responsible for the mess in my life, I was going to have to clean it up. Certainly up until that time, no one in our family did, nor did they care that my will was continually violated.

CHAPTER 6

THE BEAUTIFUL THIN LADY DISAPPEARS

For most of my early childhood,
I lived with stressful uncertainties . . .
Nothing in my life was safe, predictable, or reliable,
nor did any of life's roads for me at the time seem to make sense.

While growing up, it was confusing to try and discern all of the uncertain situations in my life which needed decoding. Days and nights were rarely consistent, and I seldom knew where I was headed, or who was going to be there, or if it might turn into a tense fight.

For most of my early childhood, I lived with stressful uncertainties, usually fearfully expecting something to go wrong, especially at night. Between my parents and grandparents, I couldn't trust their ever-changing moods, much less depend on their behavior and actions. Nothing in my life was safe, predictable, or reliable, nor did any of life's roads for me at the time seem to make sense. Uncertainty and unease ruled each day, to my utter despair.

ALCOHOL AND DRUGS

Everyone around me drank too much, and my mother and Big Red took pills regularly, causing them to be irrational at times. Big Red received injections at least once a week for her headaches. Years later, her physician told me she was addicted to tranquilizers and Demerol.

Mother and Big Red both used Paregoric to subdue and pacify me to keep me out of sight. Prescription drugs were routinely passed around by the adults in our family at both houses. They each seemed to have their own doctors to take care of them. We rarely went to a doctor's office; instead, doctors came to our house when needed. Most of the time, it was just to give someone a shot. I don't know what these shots were, but they always made my parents or grandparents feel better.

DOCTORS ON CALL

Whatever the medicinal needs of my parents and grandparents, they were met with ease. There was very little they wanted that was not granted, regardless of when or where they happened to be. Even when I was on trips with my grandparents, a doctor invariably showed up to give Big Red her shots.

MEAN AND VINDICTIVE

In thirty-four years of knowing Big Red, I never heard a kind or gracious word flow from her mouth. As Jem said in Harper Lee's novel *To Kill A Mockingbird*, "He is the meanest man that ever took a breath of life." Or better yet, "She'd just as soon shoot ya, as look at ya." Those words fit Big Red to a T.

Sadly, that's how I'll always remember Big Red. She was vindictive, hurtful, cruel, and resolutely without any kindness or compassion. All she ever did was complain and gripe about everyone, everything, and every place.

DISTURBING EVENTS

Between ages four and five, on one particular warm summer evening at the family ranch owned by my grandfather and father, I was suddenly and alarmingly awakened in the middle of the night. Actually, this happened on three separate occasions. Each of those times, I was put in the back of the 1949 Chevrolet station wagon my grandparents kept at the ranch, and we were driven across Highway 281 to an old Civilian Conservation Corps (CCC) camp, which was an outdoor rock pavilion. This CCC facility was built during the 1930s courtesy of FDR (then President Franklin Delano Roosevelt). It was a part of the family ranch.

These events took place outdoors and were usually held during the darkest hours of the night. I guess it was around midnight, and the setting was really eerie. A large bonfire was burning outside the camp pavilion upon our arrival, and it was beyond my limited understanding to know what these secretive late night meetings were all about. What I do remember most about those people in attendance is that they were mostly grown-ups who were much taller and bigger than me. I also recall seeing one of the doctors who frequently visited our home at one of those camp meetings.

They joined in chanting and performing some kind of weird ritual around a big outdoor bonfire. It was definitely abnormal and strange, at least to me, especially since all I wanted to do was go back home and go to sleep to forget this strange nightmare.

MOTHER'S COLLAPSE

I can still see Big Red's angry face peering at me with a glowering look of meanness. She gave me something bitter to drink, and it stung my mouth. I was forced to swallow the concoction, although my gut reaction was to spit it out. I have no idea what it was, nor why I was being required to drink it, but the angry glare from Big Red said it all: "Drink it or else."

When Big Red turned and walked toward Mother with the bitter drink, I saw The Beautiful Thin Lady collapse to the ground. The look of hatred on Big Red's face was worse than any horror movie I'd ever seen. The fire blazed behind her, and it cast a frightening shadow of her. Her shadow was as terrifying as the Shadow that stalked our house in the night. I tightly closed my eyes and began to hum to myself. That is all I remember of that dark night.

MOTHER'S NERVOUS BREAKDOWN

Several days later, I was returned to my parents' home in the City. I had not seen Mother since the night she fainted at the camp pavilion. It was then my Father said that The Beautiful Thin Lady was very sick, and she had been taken to a hospital in Galveston. Apparently, she'd suffered some sort of nervous breakdown; years later I learned she had undergone electric and insulin shock treatment as well as psychotherapy in the Galveston hospital. While at this institution, she was in treatment for some sort of mental and emotional disturbance, and I didn't see my mother for more than a year.

To this day, I still have no idea why I was transported to that CCC camp bonfire or what they were doing. I don't know whether these might have been some sort of clandestine KKK (Ku Klux Klan) ceremonies, or perhaps a dark devil ritual of some sort. Either way, those participating were definitely warped and twisted.

I only know that I was terrified (to the core of my being), and the presence of evil had never felt more real.

CHAPTER 7

HELP ARRIVES

*Just being with someone during the day who liked and cared
for me was a welcome change to my otherwise dreary life.*

Father was too busy with work and life outside the family to care
for us children. He would leave for the office every morning at 5
AM and stop at a local diner for breakfast. Years later, I learned that
my youngest daughter's mother-in-law had worked at this same diner
when she was younger. She said Father appeared to be a sad and lonely
person, and that image of him then certainly corresponds with mine
now.

Our household in the City was run by a maid, Dora, and a yard-
man, Willie D, whose job also included chauffeuring Brother and me.
Dora didn't really have time to care for us because her main job was to
clean house, prepare the meals, and do the laundry. So, during Mother's year-long absence, Father hired another maid to serve our family.

While interviewing for a cook, Father was also looking for someone who could take care of me as well, and so he hired Rosetta, an East Texas woman of color. She was from Marshall, Texas, and had grown to adulthood without a father or mother. As a child, Rosetta had been sent to live with an old aunt, who never considered her a part of their family. So, at age seventeen, she married Delbert, an army sergeant ten years her elder. Their first and only child, a son, passed away from pneumonia at only six months old. They decided to leave Marshall and relocate in Fort Worth. While in Marshall, Rosetta had been a short order cook at a small café, and she fit the bill perfectly for Father's purposes.

Rosetta and Delbert didn't have a place to live when they first moved to Ft. Worth. Therefore, when Father hired her, he offered them our small servants' quarters off the garage. They lived in these garage quarters for more than a year, until they bought a small house about two miles away from our home.

JOB DESCRIPTION

Father told Rosetta that Mother was not a well woman, and he needed someone to prepare family meals, but that her first priority was to take care of me. She would then share the rest of the household chores with Dora, who was assigned to see after Brother.

The household staff had their normal orders, but their duties went well beyond household cleaning and cooking chores. In our family matters, they were all priceless, because they really did care for us with heartfelt devotion! With the aid of our household staff, Brother and I were well taken care of physically, emotionally, and spiritually.

PRICELESS JEWEL

Rosetta had strong hands and I watched those hands work hard every day as she cooked, cleaned, and took care of me. She took me to the doctor, the dentist, the toy store, and shopping. Whatever I needed or wanted, Rosetta was there and always attentive. She awakened me in the mornings, dressed and fed me, and then made sure I had something to occupy my time so she could tend to other household chores.

There were some really fun days when we visited her friends, who worked as maids in other large homes on the west side of town. It was an odd feeling to go into these stately mansions lining the streets of the wealthy neighborhoods. Usually no one was at home except for other black women dressed just like Rosetta. Their maid uniforms were gray, pink, blue, or yellow, with a white collar and trim on the sleeves. Each of them also wore a white apron tied at her waist. They all smoked and wore bright red lipstick and red fingernail polish.

They all called each other "Girl," and their constant happy chatter and laughter was contagious. Most importantly, they really seemed to like me. Most of our visits with the maids in these large homes took place in the laundry rooms or kitchens. I never saw any of the owners who lived there, so I assumed they too, like my mother, were in their bedrooms.

At all of these different homes, the housemaids would usually give me a piece of cake or a Coca-Cola to drink. It was always fun to spend the day with Rosetta. Just being with someone during the day that liked and cared for me was an enjoyable change from my otherwise dreary life at home.

ROSETTA'S HUSBAND

In the evenings when Delbert arrived home from his job, I heard him coming up the steps from the garage. I greeted him eagerly at the top of the stairs with a big smile and a hug. Delbert swept me up in the air and spun me around. Then we headed inside, where he greeted Rosetta with a kiss. He then perched himself up on a yellow stool in the kitchen and enjoyed a large, refreshing glass of Rosetta's sweetened ice tea.

Delbert looked and sang like Nat King Cole, and he taught me how to dance and sing. Crooning just like a pro, Delbert sang *Blueberry Hill*, *Kansas City*, and *Mona Lisa*. My favorite song that he sang, however, was *Chantilly Lace*! I twirled around the kitchen while Rosetta prepared dinner. The kitchen smelled so delicious as there was a roast in the oven, green beans on the stove, and mashed potatoes (whipped without one lump), all fluffy and full of butter. Between the cakes, pies, chicken n' dumplings, cornbread, and greens, appetizing and healthy food was prepared and served at every meal.

GOOD COOKING

Oftentimes, I'd sneak behind Rosetta and take a bite of her tasty cake or some other dessert. Whenever I was caught, she'd say, "Shoo, you are going to ruin your dinner!" With a great big grin, I replied back, "Can't help it! You are the best cook in the whole wide world!" Then the three of us burst into laughter as she reached down and playfully nudged me in the stomach with her wooden spoon. Delbert teased his wife by singing *Unforgettable*. Rosetta put her hand on her hip and gave him a raised eyebrow. Her look said, "I do not have time for this now. Both of you stop your playing around!"

Being in the warm kitchen with the two of them was always the highlight of my day. It was fun and full of enjoyable, light conversation and acts of kindness. They were my real family, or so it seemed at the time. As a matter of fact, Rosetta and I spent so much time together that the little boy next door asked his mother one day if he could go and play with the maid's daughter.

CHAPTER 8

FAIRY GODMOTHER

Hope would transform tragedy into a story of the
faithfulness of God, and the dirge of my life would
be transformed into a song of beauty.

At nighttime, one of my greatest fears was being spotted as I walked through the living room to my bedroom at the far end of the house. There were two open arched doorways leading into the music room from the living room. If I made it past the first door, I might be lucky enough to make it past door number two. If detected, Father called out, "Carmyn, Carmyn, come in here." This meant an hour or more of what I considered "life lessons" from my alcohol-lubricated Father. He always greeted me as "my little princess." (All the princesses I had read or heard about had fairy godmothers. I kept hoping my fairy godmother would appear and magically change things. She never did!)

Frequently, the Man in Black-Rimmed Glasses prattled on endlessly about money and how I was never going to have to worry about finances because he had seen to everything. My future, I was told, had been taken care of by him. On and on, ad nauseam, he claimed my inheritance and trusts were going to provide for the rest of my life. My young mind had no idea what he was talking about, but I just sat there while he gave his "money sermon." I guess those money sermons helped him feel good about himself, but there was cold comfort in them for me.

Father's Distresses

Occasionally, Father would cry and tell me how difficult it was for him to work so hard, and how sad that his wife was not well mentally. "It runs in her family, you know," he reminded me more than once. Then, of course, logically speaking, that broad injunction would have necessarily included me. He would pull my head into his chest as he sobbed, by then well-oiled with alcohol. These moments were always very uncomfortable, and so I just sat there in silence. From the young ages of four to ten, I didn't know what to say or do to stop his crying. It was pathetic, really.

On these instructional evenings Father smelled like a bouquet of different aromas, which included a combination of Vitalis hair oil and heavy cigarette smoke. His forehead was shiny with hair oil, and he looked and felt greasy too. I rarely saw him without a lit Lucky Strike smoldering in his hand.

Music Lessons

The hidden stereo in the music room was playing most evenings. Father had a love affair with Opera, and he introduced me to the works of Bizet, Mozart, Wagner, Verdi, and Rimsky-Korsakov. We spent hours in that dimly lit and smoke-filled music room as we listened to classical symphonies and operas.

There are two things that pierce the human heart, writes Simone Weil; one is beauty and the other is affliction. Father seemed to thrive on both. While he downed Brandy from a Baccarat snifter, he explained the story behind the opera music. The orange glow of a cigarette swayed in his hand, keeping time with the music as Father hummed the haunting musical scores.

No wonder he was sad and depressed most of the time, because most stories behind the ominous opera music were generally dismal and heavy. They were not at all like the happy songs Delbert sang.

Painfully, the many demons Father struggled with all his life also served to torment me as well, as he violated my childhood innocence and God-given free will every time he abused me with his despicable drunken misbehavior.

THE PINK ROSE

At the end of an opera, the cast learns how well it has performed from the number of curtain calls prompted by the standing ovations of the audience. The lead actress is presented with a bouquet of roses, and in the case of Carmen, red roses. A red rose alone stands for and symbolizes the opera *Carmen*. Many times Father would comment on how he could imagine a red rose clenched in my mouth, with my fingers snapping and my feet tapping in Senorita style: Ole!

From this point on, very early in life, I sought another story. My heart's desire was to know only beauty, but the painful abuse of my childhood raised serious doubts whether the world I lived in held any joy and vibrancy for me. Little did I know that God had divinely implanted deep within my heart, from infancy, a song, which refused to go unheard in the resounding fury of evil perpetrators. At the right time, in the right order, and through the right means, God held a tender pink rose ready to bloom from the ashes of painful abuse. This hope would alter tragedy into a story of the faithfulness of God, and the dirge of my life would be transformed into a song of joy.

BEDTIME

If there was a song of happiness in my abused young life, it was the sweet voice of my rescuer. "OK, Miss Carmyn, it's time to get ready for bed."

At that point, beauty came to me through Rosetta, who had become the fairy godmother I longed to have.

CHAPTER 9

FORGOTTEN SON

*At the front of the sanctuary, above the altar, was a
symbol of Jesus hanging on the cross. I felt sorry
for Jesus and did not understand why He was
on the cross . . . I guessed His Father didn't like Him either.*

As a youngster, Big Red took me twice a year to the downtown Neiman Marcus department store in Dallas. She picked me up before nine in the morning and off we drove to travel the turnpike going thirty miles east to Dallas. There I was outfitted with a new apparel of clothes appropriate for the upcoming season.

Apparently, in the grand scheme of high society, it was important to be perfectly attired, including gloves, red patent Mary Jane shoes, and always a hat. Rosetta got me ready to go well before Big Red arrived. It was Red's liking to always arrive on time. Actually, a day of shopping with Big Red was always extravagant.

Upon arrival, a wardrobe consultant, Sadie, would enthusiastically greet us. Then she arranged numerous outfits from dressy to casual, panties, pajamas, coats, socks, shoes, gloves, and hats for me to try on! Being only five, I hated having to wear hats, especially some of the gaudy ones Big Red picked out. Whatever she thought was needed for each season was carefully organized in a private room. There the final selections of my new wardrobe were chosen—by Big Red, of course. Our fitting room was spacious, and it seemed more like a fancy hotel suite. As an added pleasure, the room service was really great too! On a regular basis we were served soft drinks and snacks, and it was great daytime fun for a youngster. I loved it.

Big Red's shopping regimen was to buy by the dozen: a dozen panties, socks, and leotards, all in different colors. If she really liked something, it was purchased in all available colors except brown. She despised the color brown; it reminded her of the Great Depression during the 1930s, and she felt like it was the most unflattering color a woman could wear.

After what seemed endless hours of trying on clothes, I would become tired and bored. Enough was enough. Promptly at noon, Sadie escorted us upstairs for lunch in the Zodiac Room. The Zodiac Room is a fancy café in Neiman Marcus. I was usually served a Shirley Temple, with lots of cherries and cherry juice mixed with ginger ale. The waiter also served the three of us tasty popovers with strawberry butter. The noon meal was simply scrumptious. Big Red and Sadie would gossip on and on about important people while they ate lunch. Beautiful tall and skinny ladies modeled gorgeous clothing, and I dreamed of becoming a model myself one day.

After lunch, we returned to the fitting room for Big Red to be outfitted. During her clothing session, I played house in the large dressing room. I would get Big Red's handkerchief out of her purse and pretend to dust the tables. Sadie unplugged the phone so I could make believe I was talking on it. She brought me a bag full of cosmetic samples. Shopping at Neiman Marcus was generally a long day, and I usually fell asleep on the car ride back home. My new clothes would arrive days later and then Rosetta would neatly put them away in my closet and drawers.

Part of Rosetta's job was to have my clothes ready to wear each day, and I wasn't allowed any say-so about what I wore. But the main thing I learned very early on in childhood is that it's very important how you look and especially what you wear on a daily basis.

ATTENDING CHURCH

I was brought to church maybe a dozen times a year. Father never went to church, but dropped Mother and me off on his way to the office, at about seven, on those Sunday mornings. It was an Episcopal church and Mother preferred the short communion service only. We didn't do much but stand and kneel. My knees hurt so much that I sat on the floor with my back against the pew. At the front of the sanctuary, above the altar, was a symbol of Jesus hanging on the cross. I felt sorry for Jesus and did not understand why He was on the cross. During some of the Book of Common Prayer readings, I *thought* I heard the minister quote from a book: "God gave his only forgotten Son to die on the cross." I guessed His father didn't like him either. (The Scripture reading from the prayer book actually reads "God sent His only begotton Son.")

Of course when attending church on infrequent Sundays, I had to wear a ridiculous hat, like a beret or some other funny-looking festooned creation, which was suitable for wearing to lunch at "The Club" afterward. One Easter, when about age six, I came to the breakfast table before church. We always went to church on Easter, and Brother must have been with Big Red, because I seldom remember him going to the Easter service with Mother and me. On this particular Easter, I entered the dining room dressed in my "Easter Parade" garb, but I didn't have on my Easter hat. Mother asked Rosetta, since she was the one who always dressed me, "Where is Carmyn's hat?"

I pretended like I didn't hear, but I did hear Rosetta's voice assuring Mother she had put it on me. I continued to eat and kept my head down to avoid questioning. Now the adults' search was on for my Easter bonnet. Rosetta, and even Brother's caregiver, Dora, were brought into the hunt. They looked high and low for more than thirty minutes, but they couldn't locate the dreaded Easter hat. Finally, we left for church and I got away without having to wear that stupid hat!

Days later, when Dora changed the sheets on Brother's bed, she found my hat stuffed between the mattress and box springs. Thankfully, my transgression was met with no repercussions from my parents.

For years afterward, Rosetta laughed about that silly Easter hat episode. "Child, you were not going to wear that hat, no," she laughed with her contagious and hearty chuckles as she would retell the story. From the time Rosetta came into my life at age four, I loved her like she was my own mother. She was certainly more a mother to me than my biological mother! Affectionately, I often called her Mama Rose, a secret we kept between the two of us.

CHAPTER 10

MY FIRST ROSE

*There were many racial adjustments Rosetta and I
faced as we journeyed together during my childhood.*

I'll always remember the perplexing day Rosetta and I went shopping downtown at the humongous department store. Our assignment was to buy me some pretty white panties with lace on the leg openings. The children's section of that enormous place was on the second floor, and as long as I live, I'll always remember reading the foreboding sign over the store's elevator. It read: "Coloreds use the stairs." These were common incidents in the South during the 1950s.

It met with such an affront, even to me as a small child, that I instinctively knew that Rosetta didn't want to put me on the elevator by myself. But I didn't know what to do or what could be done in the face of such an obstacle. Looking at my pale white hand, I placed it tightly in Rosetta's large dark hand. I looked up at Rosetta's perplexed expression and said, "It's OK. We'll take the stairs together." This was one of the many racial adjustments Rosetta and I faced as we journeyed together during my childhood.

As we walked through the double doors into the store's stairwell, there were two water fountains. One fountain was white, nice, and clean, but the other was dirty and unappealing. The sign above the clean water fountain read "White Only," and above the dirty fountain the sign read: "Colored."

I didn't understand why people were treated so differently because of their color. Rosetta cared for and loved me more than any white adult I'd ever been around. Even at my young age I knew that the dastardly practice of differentiating between two races was hateful, wrong, and mean.

BODY BRUISES

At times when I was returned home from Big Red's, there would be fresh bruises and other red marks indicating physical abuse on different parts of my body. Rosetta would undress me for a bath, gasp at the sight of those new bruises and trauma signs, and then pull me close to her bosom. She rocked me back and forth. "Oh baby, my sweet baby," she cried as she rocked me. And then, Rosetta moaned her familiar "Ummm, mmm . . . uhmmmm . . . " It was clear she found it hard to let me go with Big Red to the Ranch, but we both knew there was nothing she could do about that.

Big Red always said, "They are just hired help! Servants." And that was one of the nicest things she said about the maids, even though they faithfully took care of our every need. She and my grandfather treated our domestic help harshly, and spoke terrible words about, those who, time and time again, graciously served and responded to their every call. I cringed every time my grandparents used the "N" word when referring to their dutifully faithful employees. My grandparents were routinely ungrateful, discourteous, and disrespectful to their help!

ROSETTA'S CARE, BACKGROUND

Many times from ages four to eight, Rosetta held me close and sang sweet songs to offset some of the bad things happening in my young life. Things that happened at night that no child should ever have to suffer and endure. Things that were degrading, sinful, and full of shame.

Rosetta told me stories of her own growing-up years, of the prejudices and injustices that came simply because of her skin color. Not only did whites treat her mean, her own parents didn't want her. She was sent to live with an aunt, and even then, Rosetta's aunt said she wasn't wanted at their home either. But since nobody else wanted her, Rosetta was forced to live with the family, under difficult conditions. Her aunt made it clear that she was not considered part of their family, and so poor Rosetta was not allowed to sleep in their house. She slept on a side porch with the dogs.

Those days and nights when I would cry from the sting of Mother's hurtful and cruel remarks, like a soothing balm Rosetta would cuddle me close, saying, "Oh child, your mama just don't know how to love you. She's sick, but it's not your fault, baby; it's not your fault. You got to be strong for Mama Rose, you hear?" Rosetta comforted me like no one else could, because we both knew the pain and humiliation of rejection, as well as outright denial by our own families. That pain of family rejection, common to us both, bonded us together in a way that was steadfast and unshakeable.

FAITH IN GOD

Rosetta's faith in God was very strong. She was a living example of that spiritual dimension of life that I needed so desperately. Otherwise, there was no hope of escape from the white adults in my life. There, in her arms, I felt safe when Rosetta hummed the old gospel song *What a Friend We Have in Jesus*, which I also heard when she took me to her church. I usually cried and sniffled myself fitfully to sleep as Rosetta rocked me back and forth in her nurturing embrace.

By the time I was six, Delbert and Rosetta had moved into their own home about two miles from our house. Sadly, a year or two after moving, Delbert died from cancer. What a shock! This was my first encounter with death. I couldn't really grasp what had just happened, but I knew it was awful for Rosetta. Father drove me over to Rosetta's house. She was lying in bed weeping. I walked over to an open window. The pink, ruffled curtains gently swayed in the breeze. I longed to get in bed and cry with her, because I wanted to comfort her.

Delbert's death was the first traumatic bereavement I'd ever experienced firsthand. I knew nothing I could say or do would make Rosetta's grief go away. I felt her pain and stood there with my back to Rosetta as tears rolled down my cheeks too. My heart ached in a way I'd never known before, but I didn't know how to comfort my sweet Mama Rose.

THE ROSE IN ROSETTA

And while I didn't understand Rosetta's God, I listened with rapt attention every time she prayed. God heard those prayers, as I discovered later in life, much later, as God kept her prayers stored in heaven to come to fulfillment in the hour of my greatest need.

And so, my first true rose in life was Rosetta. Her name says it all! She had and always will have a warm and precious place in my heart and life, forever. My own true blessed rose, Rosetta represented for me then—and now—hope for the future and a way to endure the present.

CHAPTER 11

A FIELD OF DAISIES

Here alone, in my field of daisies, I dreamed of a different life.

For some, childhood memories bring recollections of carefree days playing with toys, swinging outdoors and trying to touch the sky with tiny bare feet, or maybe playing with dolls on a rainy day indoors, with the family cat as the honored guest for tea. Or perhaps they bring thoughts of enjoying warm homemade cookies with grandma. And the incomparable feeling on a stormy night of being held in the gentle arms of a father while he reads *The Chronicles of Narnia* to you, fearing nothing but the end of the chapter and time for bed.

The memories of happier times with Rosetta are the ones I cherish most. However, most of my memories of childhood are dark and unpleasant, filled with hurtful episodes of abuse and mistreatment. I felt crushed by adult caretakers who cared only for their own pleasures, pursued, it seems in reflection, largely at my expense. My childhood seemed to consist of one episode after another of oppression at the hands of my abusers. Desperate to find something or someone to save me, I ran frantically in search of a knight in shining armor. While I didn't know it then, that rescue would happen much later in my life.

From about three years young, I was forced to run from a monster, and more times than not, I was caught, and Big Red was my monster. She was a hate-filled, anger-driven woman.

TIMES AT THE RANCH

I remember being afraid and fearful of being alone in the 1940s white frame Ranch house, whether in early mornings, mid-afternoons during the hot Texas summers, or on cold days in the winter. Whenever I had to make that dreaded trip to the Ranch with Big Red, my stomach churned with fear. I knew that unless my adult-avoidance maneuvers were successful, in all likelihood, bad things were in store for me.

One summer afternoon in the mid-1950s while down at the Ranch, I looked for Big Red to ask if I could get something out of the fridge to drink. Since I was unable to find her in the usual place, which was sitting on the chaise lounge in the sunroom, I looked in her bedroom just off the stairs. The door had been closed, but when I opened it I saw Boots, the ranch foreman, and Big Red standing together partially disrobed.

That day marked a new escalation of Big Red's cruel punishments for my untimely intrusion into her bedroom at the Ranch. And so, from that day on, whenever I heard Boots's pickup truck come down the road, I darted faster than a jackrabbit out of the ranch house. Fearing punishment, I ran through the dining room and then out the kitchen door. This was my getaway escape route to the pasture. I was terrified at the prospect of Big Red's or Boots's hand snatching me by the nape of my neck or shirt, as would surely happen if my frantic exit was noticed while in progress.

ESCAPE TO THE PASTURE

Outside the fenced-in backyard, my little feet ran as fast as they could carry me across the rocked patio, onto the grass, and through the gate. Then I hurried down the beaten path that led to the servants' quarters. If I could see around the corner of the house that the coast was clear, I was almost assured of making it to my intended destination.

One more final scoot under the rectangular metal gate and I was out of hearing range. Finally, I reached my treasured sanctuary space in the pasture . . . my fortress, the hidden brush and native grasses among the live oak and mesquite trees. This was my ultimate hiding place and a treasured place of safety from the cruel reaches of my tormentors.

By this time, my heart was pounding like a jackhammer and I felt the pulse in my neck and chest beating wildly, but it gave me a rush of accomplishment. I had escaped the monster without being caught. Now I was safe and sound at least for the moment, away from yelling and the tight handgrip of an angry adult clenched around my neck.

If I hadn't made it this far untouched, I would have found my head being forced down and held underneath the water in a cattle trough until I was breathless. My face was plunged beneath the dirty water's surface over and over again, while being threatened within inches of my life if I ever breathed a word about what I'd seen. Such was the angry chastisement for a small helpless child who had unintentionally interfered with Big Red and Boots's secret sexual activities.

In the safety of my sanctuary pasture, wildflowers grew that looked like tiny daisies. They were white, with pretty yellow centers, and this was my safe haven, this field of daisies. Here I could lie down in the midst of soft flowers, look up, and see the vast blue sky overhead. Finally I felt safe for the moment, buried in their welcome arms, tiny and unseen and free for the time being. This was my temporary refuge from adult torment where I could rest, untrampled and undiscovered.

Here alone in my field of daisies I dreamed of a different life.

CHAPTER 12

MORE RANCH INCIDENTS

*I kept my fears and pain hidden within; there was no one
in my family that could be trusted.*

Stories of escaping from the dysfunctional oppressor-adults in my life entertained my mind in the sanctuary of the pasture, and my daydreams of living and being elsewhere would entertain me for hours. Sometimes I was a heroine rescuing a dog or other children from harm's way. I pretended being Shirley Temple and playacting her movie roles. I imagined I was a beautiful ballerina, dancing on clouds in the sky. One of my favorite daydreams was to be an ice-skater, and I would glide, jump, and do spins while adorned in beautiful blue costumes.

I lay for endless hours in this ranch pasture sanctuary, daydreaming and even sleeping. It was exhausting trying to outwit the adults in my life. But there in the field of daisies, I imagined a beautiful world where life was happy and full of laughter. In the gentle breezes, faintly,

I heard a sweet voice calling me to a better life somewhere out there. The music was Judy Garland's song *Somewhere Over the Rainbow*. I longed for such a place, where tiny little bluebirds sang, far, far away.

THE FALL AT THE RANCH

Big Red's habit was to jerk, pull, or shove me in the direction she wanted me to go. Her flat hand striking me angrily would cause the deepest feelings of shame and embarrassment to redden my face. She would raise her arm and swing, hitting my cheek with such force it knocked me off my feet. (The Beautiful Thin Lady slapped me too, but she was not nearly as strong as Big Red.)

Once, when I was age five, Big Red yanked me upstairs to be locked in my designated bedroom there at the Ranch. When I fiercely resisted her, she pulled her hand back and hit me so hard at the top of the stairs that I hit the door frame and fell down the stairs all the way to the bottom. Ellen, Big Red's maid, came running when she heard all the commotion. She found me at the bottom of the stairs lying unconscious . . . and still.

Mother, Rosetta and Ellen related this story to me several times during my childhood. They said Big Red had panicked after seeing what she'd done. My nose was bleeding and Ellen was left to clean up my face while Big Red called our house in the city to let them know I'd had a bad fall and she was driving me back. It was an hour's drive from the Ranch to my house, and when we got there I was still unconscious. Big Red rang the doorbell, and when Rosetta and Mother answered, she handed me to them and then left without any explanation. Obviously, Big Red assumed no responsibility for this injurious incident. Even worse, from my perspective, neither parent attempted to hold her accountable, nor even questioned the "accident" circumstances.

Rosetta and Mother took me to the Boulevard Hospital. I'd suffered a concussion, and the right side of my cheek and nose were badly bruised. This hospital was a small private hospital owned by a group of doctors that our family always used.

BOYS PREFERRED

"We didn't want little girls; we wanted boys," Big Red always said.

She had no nurturing touch where girls were concerned in her family.

But I liked being a girl, and I didn't want to be a boy. And being a girl, I didn't have to go into Red's bedroom at night to sleep. At the Ranch, she had twin beds side by side in her bedroom. Big Red usually slept in the bed by the door and the other bed was against the wall. She always took my brother to the bedroom with her, and I was sent upstairs. I was always scared of Big Red's room because that's where I'd caught her and the ranch foreman together.

DARK NIGHT'S JOURNEY

During the times I was with my parents at the Ranch, life wasn't any better. Heated arguments would usually occur when my parents were drinking, which was often and normal. Those arguments always seemed to center on Big Red and money. Those marital face-offs became so heated that they threw things and yelled at each other. One particular hot summer night around midnight Mother stormed off to the car, with Father following right behind her. They drove the seventy-plus miles back to our home at reckless, breakneck speed, arguing the whole way. They didn't notice I'd slipped into the backseat while they were yelling. Father screamed, "You're going to kill us! You're driving too fast. Pull over!"

It drove me crazy, and I had no way of knowing what was too fast, but it was certainly frightening. Finally, Mother pulled the car over to the side of the pitch-dark highway so a less intoxicated parent could finish the drive home. When the car door opened, I feared Mother was going to drive off and leave Father abandoned in the night. Not that I cared if I ever saw him again, but I wasn't sure I could get us home from there. These sudden outbursts of anger between Mother and Father happened frequently between my ages of five and seven. When she did let Father drive, I was afraid Mother would jump out of the speeding car, so I slipped my right hand through the side of the front passenger seat and kept it firmly on the door handle.

Once home, I emptied the car of the luggage and locked the back door when all were safely inside. By then, Mother had locked the door to her bedroom, and Father was passed out on one of the twin beds in Brother's room. I got the pillow from my bedroom and slept outside Mother's bedroom door. I pretended to be a watchman in order to wake Father if Mother tried to leave. However, the real reason for sleeping on the floor in the hallway was that if Father woke up and went to my room, I wouldn't be there. I wasn't really sure whether I'd been noticed during this episode, but I didn't want to take the chance.

BROTHER UNAWARE

Since Brother slept in Big Red's room at the Ranch, I never knew if he was aware of all the hostility and conflict between our parents. But I did know that Big Red hated Mother more than me and spoke ill of her at every opportunity to anyone who would listen.

Brother and I didn't speak much about these things. I guess we'd been kept separate so much that we just didn't have a reason to talk about it with each other; we both lived in our separate worlds of inner turmoil. So we continued to act as if this conflictual lifestyle was normal. I kept all my fears, family secrets, and pain hidden within. There was no one in my family that could be trusted. I certainly believed and felt that no one cared about me, and so, I believed, this was my normal life. Thus, I learned to navigate my way through the tangled messes always present in my daily life.

CHAPTER 13

BOOGIE WOOGIE BLUES

Life had become one survival tactic after another.

By the time I was six, life had become one survival tactic after another. However, during the school year, when home with Rosetta, I'd have some fun times just being a child.

In the midst of this dark life of hidden secrets, I was able to find some bright glimpses of fun and freedom in being, intermittently, a carefree youngster like others. Three neighboring families were particularly nice; they included the girl across the street and the twin boys who lived behind us. I felt like a regular neighborhood kid when the four of us played together.

In the summer of 1955, there was a life-sized dollhouse that had been built especially for me. This dollhouse had a covered porch and windows along the sides. It had furniture inside, and the four of us spent hours playing in there. Next door to my dollhouse was a log cabin built for my brother. When he played with the twin boys' older brother, they raided my dollhouse, but it was all done in good fun.

One day, my Brother and the twins' brother got us to play circus with them. They drew a huge circle on the side of my playhouse and threw darts at me! But even worse, they put an apple on one twin's head, and his older brother shot at it with a real bow and arrow. This did not end well. The metal-tipped arrow landed right in the middle of his forehead. He turned pale white, and we walked him into the house where our parents were having their cocktail hour. At first they just laughed, but soon they realized the severity of the injury and took him to the hospital. A fourth of an inch more and the skull-piercing arrow would have killed him.

There were many close calls like this growing up. It's a miracle any of us made it to adulthood. Proper adult supervision certainly did not play a part in our existence.

THE DAY OF THE BAT

Growing older, I became interested in sports, and by age ten I was already at least a head taller than my classmates. Because of my size and height, I also had great muscle power for someone my age. Therefore, I could kick the soccer ball further, throw the football better, and hit the baseball as well as most boys in my class. A false belief emerged that I was as good in sports as any boy, which led to a disastrous event one sunny spring day.

Brother and a few of the neighborhood boys were playing baseball in our backyard. Having nothing better to do that day, I decided to join in their game. Unfortunately, I didn't take Brother's adamant "no." After an exchange of yeses and nos, Brother finally had had it with me, and he raised the baseball bat and smashed it upon my head. Immediately, I went down for the count. I have no recollection of what happened following this head-bashing incident, except Brother won and I didn't get to play baseball that day. I certainly learned not to confront Brother on any other matter after his adamant response to my request.

Brother even had the audacity, years later, to send the offending weapon of choice back to me by way of my five-year-old daughter. She excitedly walked into our home, bat in hand, and innocently held it up, not knowing its significance to me. She said, "Uncle told me to bring this to you. He said, 'Ask your mother if she remembers it.'"

I bent down so she could feel the pecan-size knot still on the top of my head, a stark reminder of that malicious incident that I bear to this day.

"Yes, how could I forget?"

"Wow, I'll bet he got into trouble for that!"

"Not that I am aware of," I replied.

To myself, I thought: *But I did learn a lesson.* From that day on, I resolved to do whatever was necessary to stay on Brother's good side. That harsh jolt seemed to define my subordinate role in life relative to my Brother, and that was to last for a long time to come.

WILLIE D

Willie D was such a clown! Occasionally he would dust the furniture for Rosetta or Dora. The Beautiful Thin Lady had a fetish for her array of "what-nots." That's what Willie D called them.

One day Willie D got a ruler and measured the exact location of the vase or box on each display table so that he could put the "what-nots" back in their exact place. I laughed and laughed at him. He looked at me with his forefinger over his lips. "Shhh . . . lawdy, Miss Carmyn, don't let yo mutter hear us. That woman can hear a gnat pee on cotton!"

Once, Willie D and I moved a statue to another knickknack display table, and lo and behold, Mother spotted it the moment she walked through the living room. Her perfectionist tendencies concerning room and furniture arrangements were an obsession!

Willie D could play the piano by ear, and he was especially good at playing the *Boogie Woogie Blues*! When The Beautiful Thin Lady was at the hairdresser, doctor, or wherever she went on those days when she left her room, Willie D played the piano while I accompanied with song and dance. To this day, I'm thankful for the wonderful musical rhythms I learned from Willie and Rosetta's husband, Delbert. They were a refreshing source of enjoyment in a world that seemed to hold little fun.

Attending Grade School

Willie D drove me to school when Rosetta couldn't. I never felt embarrassed when Rosetta took me to school because she always took me in her 1957 Chevrolet Impala. It was bright yellow with white-fin taillights, and I considered her my surrogate mother. But when Willie D took me, he always drove me in the big Cadillac. I didn't like him driving me anywhere, and I was so embarrassed by the ostentatious Caddy and, also, by being dropped off at school by a chauffeur. I was already being teased for being a "poor little rich girl," and this just made a humiliating situation worse.

Four blocks from school, I demanded Willie D let me out of the car. Then I could walk the rest of the way and arrive at school without evident embarrassment. Of course, I pretended not to know who was following me in that Cadillac with the passenger's side window rolled down as I walked along the sidewalk. Willie D wanted to make sure I got to school safely, but I just wanted him to go away so I could be like everyone else; instead, I felt like the emperor with no clothes amid the snickering of other observing students.

CHAPTER 14

THE BIG "C"

There wasn't much healthy about my growing up . . .
I was definitely the misfit of the family.

I learned how to drive automobiles on a standard-shift 1949 Chevrolet station wagon kept at the ranch when I was eight. I eventually got to where I could drive this car, as well as others, really well. Off I drove whenever I could around the rough dirt roads coursing in the mesquite and cedar-filled pastures. At age ten I was sometimes successful in persuading a reluctant Willie D to let me drive to school so I wouldn't be embarrassed. Amazing! Even the kids at school thought that was pretty cool!

Between ages eight and ten, while at the ranch, I was allowed to drive the old 1949 Chevrolet. It was a wood-paneled station wagon. To the east of the main ranch house was a gate into an adjoining pasture. I would drive through this entry gate and into the adjoining five pastures, making a two-mile semicircle around the main ranch house.

I made that drive time several times a day to keep myself entertained. My vivid imagination made up all sorts of tales in my mind. That station wagon became a covered wagon that I led across the dangerous territory, just like on some of the TV westerns I occasionally watched. To this day I believe the creative side of me was birthed in those lone moments of entertaining myself to find intermittent respites of fun and peace. Anyway, Big Red was glad to have me out of the way for the day.

There was another, separate gate that led into two other pastures. This last pasture wound around onto the highway. This highway represented freedom and a way to get to the small town nine miles from the ranch. As I explored my newfound freedom, I'd drive the old station wagon and sneak it out onto highway. Every small town in Texas has a Dairy Queen! I headed that car north to drive the nine miles for one of DQ's famous soft-serve ice cream cones. What a blast!

CAUGHT ON THE HIGHWAY

This unauthorized, underage vehicular driving on the highway stopped suddenly one day, to my great chagrin. This was the day I passed my grandfather in his big white Cadillac while he was speeding down that highway. He whipped his Caddy around to follow me back to the ranch house, and man, was he furious. Grandfather grabbed me out of that old beat-up station wagon and asked if I knew having a wreck with another car might cause him to be sued to high heaven.

He didn't care that anything injurious might happen to his granddaughter. But his money . . . that was the most important thing in his life, the almighty dollar!

After that little driving mishap, the pasture gate to the highway was secured with a lock. No more trips to the Dairy Queen, but I still got to drive around the ranch pastures for hours, making complete circles in the surrounding ranch pastures. There were about 12,000 acres of ranch land owned and leased by my grandfather and father for their sideline cattle operations.

FATHER'S BUSINESSES

Father's employees would usually hold a company Christmas party at his downtown office in the city each year. He was the only son of a prominent, wealthy family. He held executive rank in seven companies, with business interests ranging from dairy products to oil and gas, from ranching to banking. In other words, his business interests were well-diversified, and he was generally considered a successful businessman, as well as being a respected citizen in the Fort Worth community.

Most years at the office Christmas party, Father was pretty well inebriated when it came time to go home. When I was nine, one of the margarine plant employees called our house, spoke to my mother, and said someone needed to come and pick him up. We all knew instantly it was because he was drunk and therefore incapable of safe driving. But Mother was in her own wonderland on a mix of Valium and alcohol, and since Rosetta had already left for the evening, I was handed the keys to the Cadillac. "Go get your father at the office," was all Mother said.

I'd ridden in this car often with my father on his way to work, so I was familiar with the route to his office on the brick boulevard that led into downtown. It was easy for me to remember. Car keys in hand, off I went, feeling totally confident by this time with driving a car, even in downtown traffic. Even though I was only nine, I was tall for my age and didn't even need to sit on a seat cushion in order to see over the steering wheel.

When I stopped the car at Father's office, the looks on the faces of the employees who delivered my father to the car said it all—but what were they going to say to the boss's daughter? With my drunken father in hand, I headed home. The whole way back to our house, Father cried and talked about what wonderful people he had working for him at the plant. The office employees always gave him such a nice gift each Christmas, and this year, 1958, they had given him a sporty 20-gauge shotgun. It, too, was part of the precious cargo on the backseat of the car.

Today, as I write this, I wonder what a policeman would have said or done if he had stopped us. Maybe he'd have found a better place for me, but I doubt it. Too many times I'd seen Father or Grandfather reach in their wallets and give police officers money. It seemed as though there wasn't anything or anyone my family couldn't buy. This was not exactly a healthy way to grow up, but then there wasn't much healthy about my upbringing anyway.

INDEPENDENCE AND ADOLESCENCE

I was now maturing, at least physically, into adolescence. However, I was an independent yet unwanted child, accustomed to doing things on my own. But predictably, I was too dependent on the power and its alluring privileges that money gave me. Innately, I liked it that we always had first-class service and other status perks that only money could buy. Soon enough I'd learn to turn my dependency on money into a source for blackmail on the one person I disliked the most . . . my father.

At the young age of nine, my breasts were growing fuller, and by the end of my fourth-grade year when I was almost ten, they were almost full size. A grade-school classmate friend held her birthday party at a roller-skating rink, and because I loved to skate I felt very adept at this particular fun activity, so I couldn't wait to go. The day of the party Rosetta came into my room, but when she opened the door I was in the corner of my bedroom with the draperies drawn and the lights out. I declared to her that I wasn't going to the party. She asked what the matter was, and I told her that I was dying of cancer. Rosetta tried hard to keep from laughing, but politely inquired, "Why do you think you have cancer?"

"I'm bleeding." It was thoroughly frightening to be in what I assumed was an alarming physical ailment. As was the case in my family, bodily functions were not mentioned, so naturally I hadn't been forewarned about this transitional female entrance into womanhood.

Father came home that evening, heard the news, and declared me to be a woman. He seemed to take great delight in sharing the biology of what had happened. It was humiliating for my father to be the one to deliver this distasteful explanation about a woman's menstrual cycle. Rosetta had given me this horrible belt and pad to wear, which was, to me, an ultimate badge of shame. Amazingly, the Beautiful Thin Lady never said a word about this disgusting, not to mention embarrassing, hallmark of entry into adolescence.

Cancer would have been easier, I thought to myself. Did boys have to do this? No, certainly not! Maybe I should have been a boy after all.

SELF-MUTILATION

By now I'd learned a sort of palliative anesthetic to painful childhood experiences, which, strangely enough, seemed to make things a bit easier to handle. When life events were too much for me to abide, not having anyone to explain unhappy occurrences which kept on repeating themselves, I would run out to an open field down the street from our house and cut myself. I would use a broken piece of glass on my legs and watch myself bleed. From age seven, this had become a habitual practice, so it didn't seem strange to do this, and somehow, it relieved some of the pain I was feeling. My usual excuse, when anyone asked what had happened, was that I had fallen into a rosebush and the thorns had scratched my skin in several places.

This self-mutilation practice would continue until I was sixteen, but later progressed to more flagrant acts of hurting myself. I'd scraped rocks across my face and arms at age fifteen, but everyone believed my story of being in a motorcycle accident. Then I pounded an iron rod on my ankle, and everyone believed I'd fallen and sprained my ankle. Habitual lying, with made-up stories of friends and places I'd been to, and other ridiculous tales, had become the norm. I was desperate to find acceptance and approval but was known as an emotionally unstable and unruly child. By this time, I was definitely the misfit of the family.

CHAPTER 15

DOWNWARD SPIRAL

I felt awkward and out of place with kids my own age.
I became increasingly self-conscious about my body size and height.

Childhood had drastically changed by the time I turned ten. I don't know exactly why, but I felt awkward and out of place with kids my own age. Part of it had to do with my early-maturing body, but a lot of it was due to the fact that no one in my family cared about me or who or what I was becoming. I had drifted away from my old group of friends and was isolating myself. At the same time, my body morphed, and by age twelve I was already five-foot-ten, taller than most of the boys in my class. Naturally, I was uncomfortable when passing a table of boys in the lunchroom, as they would "Moo" at me because of my large breasts. I became increasingly self-conscious of my body size and height.

In this new era of development and on the verge of being a teen-ager, I was the only girl in my class who wore high heel pumps, a garter belt, and hose. Most of my friends were still in Mary Janes and white lace socks. So I continued to feel odd and different from others my age. I didn't fit in, and it was awkward for everyone, especially me. Particularly since most of the mothers of my school classmates would not allow their girls to socialize with me. Who could blame them? Certainly not me: at my age I didn't fit the typical fifth-grade schoolgirl image.

LITTLE WOMAN

The Man in Black-Rimmed Glasses continued to be proud of his "little woman." From time to time he'd touch my shoulder and say, "You are becoming such a beautiful young woman." Most girls long to hear such complimentary remarks from their fathers, but this was different, and I sensed instinctively that it was wrong and impure. I had a creepy feeling as his dark eyes scanned my body and he caressed my face. This abnormal behavior toward me became increasing uncomfortable for me in my newly blossoming body. Somehow, I sensed more troubles ahead, but then, based on earlier experiences, why would I not?

SOCIAL GRACES

By now I was enrolled in ballroom dancing lessons. I was being primed for the upcoming social events for young teens. The Cotillion Dance was coming soon to my age group, and so Big Red made sure Mother sent me to etiquette classes at Neiman Marcus. This was deemed important so that I'd learn the fine art of social graces. I was schooled in the proper table-setting placements and the correct dinnerware for each course. Also, I learned how to correctly sit, walk, and smile. Who knew there were so many rules to these apparently important social graces? Deep inside, I wished these outward appearance classes would just teach me how to talk and carry on a normal conversation with others. While I was being outfitted with the proper clothing and manners, I didn't know what to say or how to converse with others in social settings.

There were also weekly trips to the beauty salon to have my hair styled, and for manicures and pedicures. By now, I was becoming accustomed to these social indulgences.

THE DOCTOR'S OFFICE AND THE NIGHTMARE

Then came a moment in my life that changed everything; with this new body of mine came a horrible and unsettling new experience. My monthly periods stopped. I didn't complain; I was glad not to have to wear the uncomfortable belt and pad.

However, one morning Big Red arrived out of the blue to take me to see a doctor. No one asked any questions and least of all me. She demanded absolute authority and no one stood in her way. Once we were at the doctor's office, I was told to put on a robe. After putting the robe on, a nurse came in and led me to a room with a long metal table with a large bright light hanging over it. This steel table was cold and hard, but all I remember was something resembling a strainer with a cloth over it was placed over my mouth and nostrils. I was forced to breathe in a horrible smell, and now I know it was the anesthetic, ether.

While unconscious, I dreamed that I was falling downward in a spiral, and at the end of this spinning spiral of black and orange was a funny little man with a huge hat on. He was laughing and saying repeatedly, "You'll never get out. You'll never get out." The words pounded and reverberated in my head until I was afraid I'd never wake up and be trapped in that place forever. It was one of the most frightening experiences of my life.

Upon awakening, I suddenly realized that I was back at Big Red's house in the room with no windows. I didn't understand what had just taken place, but my period was back and I bled for several days.

I never asked why or what had happened to me on that cold steel table, and I had no real understanding about it until years later.

CHAPTER 16

MOTHER'S RESURRECTION

From my perspective, it was too little, too late . . .

Between ages twelve and thirteen, Mother finally became sober. She became the belle of the ball in alcohol-recovery society and did volunteer work with Alcoholics Anonymous. At the height of her social notoriety, she sold programs for the Junior League and was invited to join a very prestigious women's social club. A really big deal was made about her membership acceptance into this prestigious group. With that announcement came floral bouquets by the dozens, it seemed, with congratulatory notes from the group's members, and our phone rang off the wall.

I know this will be hard to believe, but the Beautiful Thin Lady had an incredibly charming personality and everyone in polite society loved her. She had a great sense of humor, was witty, and very generous with her money. Mother went out of her way to entertain my friends, saying, "Darling, can I get you something to drink?" as she was eager to impress them. I hated it that she called all my friends "Darling"! My friends never knew Mother was a completely different, cold, and hypercritical person when they were not around.

DISTANT DAD

Father was a different story, and my friends were afraid of him. He was a successful businessman, but his mere presence alone subliminally said, "I am not to be reckoned with. Leave me alone." He was not a warm person. Father somehow managed to put on a good show of courteous behavior at social events. But then, all of our family members knew how to wear our masks in public.

Father was distant and detached, especially to us family members. He was a worrier and seldom did one see a smile on his face unless he was drinking, and then he became effusively emotional, sentimental, and cried.

Regularly throughout the week, Father would pass out on the sofa in the music room at home following the conclusion of each nightly drinking episode. At this point in their marriage, Mother was completely turned off by Father, and so if not actually asleep, she pretended to be. Father was so pathetic, banging into things and stumbling around in the house late at night. What a miserable existence!

MOTHER'S CONFIDENCES

With Mother being sober and feeling better, she confided in me, telling me how horrible her marriage had been all these years, and how it still was so bad. She related what it was like being a wife to someone who was always drunk and who couldn't meet her sexual needs—things I really didn't want to know or hear.

To this day, I have no idea why the two of them stayed together. I heard repeatedly from both parents how hard it was for each to live with the other. They didn't want answers or advice; they just wanted to spew their toxic waste on an unwilling listener such as me. I couldn't express to either of them that not only did I not care, I didn't want to know about their disturbing marital problems.

THE NEW MOTHER

I hated being around the new Mother, because along with her sobriety she now found it necessary to try and have a meaningful role in my life. From my perspective, this meager effort was too little, too late. How dare her attempt to come into my life now and want to control everything. She constantly criticized my hair, how I walked and talked, and basically anything having to do with my appearance.

Actually, Mother was now competing with me on looks. While she said she wanted to be my friend, we had little in common, as too much time and too many hurtful incidents in the past prevented our becoming close. We were literally like two ships passing in the night. There could be no reconnection now to make up for the many years of lost time, with her attendant cruel, barbed, and hateful remarks and unrestrained insults.

In reality, I wanted and needed a mother, but Mother had let too much time pass for that to become her new role with me. Rosetta and I were close and always had been, but now Mother resented our relationship. For eight years Rosetta had run our household, and now Mother was trying to take over. She bossed our household help and demanded much of their time and energy. It was something like a war zone, but without a truce.

CONFLICTED RELATIONSHIP

Because my relationship with Mother was one of constant conflict, Rosetta got caught in the crossfire. I longed for Rosetta to take my side in these hurtful arguments, but she was paid help. It was not her place to take sides, and sadly, I began to pull away from Rosetta too. She still tried to give helpful advice, but now I saw her as the enemy also. It felt like there was an adult conspiracy designed to keep me from enjoying life.

I talked back to Mother, resenting that she was trying to change the familiarities in my life. We got into heated arguments that ended in shouting matches. She was anything but loving to me; a slap across my face was common for almost anything I said or did. Her favorite item to beat me with was a stiff nylon brush, which was used as punishment on my already black and blue legs.

I never knew a mother and daughter could dislike and hold such hostility toward each other. Actually we had a similar relationship as that between Mother and Big Red. It seemed like I was a constant threat and thorn in her life. Mother resented that I could charge anything to Father, who never got mad or denied any of my expensive and extravagant lifestyle choices.

CHAPTER 17

"GOT TAKEOFF"

Willie D called my new car "Got Takeoff."
And that's exactly what I did —as often, and as far away,
as possible!

For Christmas in 1963, when I was only fourteen, Big Red and my Grandfather told me to go pick out any car I wanted at the Pontiac dealership. Of course I selected a standard shift, four-on-the-floor, two-door coupe Pontiac GTO. Willie D called it "Got Takeoff." And that's exactly what I did—as often, and as far away, as possible.

About this time, one afternoon when Father was playing golf at The Club with his comrades, two cars raced down the street along the fairway by the first tee, honking loudly. One golfing crony said, "Look at those crazy kids driving so recklessly. They're going to kill themselves!"

Father nonchalantly replied, between putts on the first green, "Yeah, and one of those crazy kids is mine." But my parents were happy for me to be out of their hair, and there were no repercussions at home.

THE BLUE BIRD TAVERN

As our family conflicts continued, a deeply embedded personal hatred within my soul began to ravage me with feelings of guilt and shame. I'd been legally driving since age thirteen, and at age fourteen I had a car. During the early 1960s the age in Texas to be a licensed driver was age fourteen, but in some cases a hardship driver's license was given at age thirteen. I came and went from home as I pleased. By this time I was drinking, smoking, and going to the Blue Bird Tavern, a black nightclub close to Rosetta's house. I believed the patrons and staff liked me there, and so I felt safe there. It was fun as I played pinball, smoked, and drank beer. I enjoyed listening to the incredible jazz, blues, and singing. The songs played on the piano reminded me of the *Boogie Woogie Blues* that Willie D played. I felt much more at home there than at the Beautiful Thin Lady's house.

My grandfather sometimes drove up to the Blue Bird, got out of his Caddy, and went inside with a gun under his belt. He'd go out with some guy, but I never figured out what they were doing. Grandfather was so feared that I had no reason to feel unsafe in my surroundings there.

THE GUYS

In general, people thought me much older than thirteen, and I became aware that boys really liked to look at me (that is, my body). Naturally, I was a flirt and wore tight skirts, high heels, and dark red lipstick. Inevitably, it seemed, I attracted the wrong type of male attention and companions. Most of these newfound friends liked to drink and smoke, as did I. There was no pressure to have sex at this time and even the very thought of it was revolting to me. I wanted to be accepted and liked, and the boys seemed to enjoy just being around me. I made them laugh with my jokes and all of them were impressed I could handle my liquor. Boys were my best friends, but I kept romance at a distance. I didn't trust men, as the only ones I'd known until then were drunks or perverts, or so it seemed.

SECRET LONGINGS

It was obvious that Mother didn't like me, and although I didn't like her either, secretly I longed for her love and approval. I felt like a failure in her eyes and knew I'd never be good enough or smart enough to suit her, but did know I was pretty enough, because beauty was the one thing my parents complimented me on.

However, the compliments were always in the presence of others, never to me alone, so I felt like an accessory for them to show off.

APPEARANCES MATTER

As Mother invested more and more, at least in terms of dollars, in enhancing my appearance, it became more and more important for me to have all the "right" things and to look "perfect" at all times. My closets looked like a ladies' clothing store, packed with the latest styles and modern outfits. She loved showing me off in public wearing all the latest styles and, at thirteen, I dressed like Jackie Kennedy, the President's wife.

One outfit I remember in particular was a light gray two-piece suit. It was worn with a red, wide-brimmed hat, four-inch high heels, and red leather gloves. This was how I dressed to fly to Hawaii for a family vacation. That summer in Hawaii, I told the guys and girls at the beach that I was twenty. They believed me, until my brother announced that I was only thirteen!

REAPPEARANCE OF THE SHADOW

By now, The Shadow was brazen enough to come into my bedroom before the lights were out. He came in my room sipping his brandy and staring at my body. If I had my robe on, he would say, "Let me see your beautiful shoulders." (Why couldn't I say "No" to The Shadow, like I did with the juvenile and immature boys?) I hated that and I hated myself for unwillingly succumbing to his despicable, intrusive invasions. I felt helpless, like an indisposed hostage, to Father's sordid existence. Father continued to violate my will, and I felt powerless to stop him.

SECOND TRIP

In the spring of 1962, just before I turned thirteen, my periods stopped again, but this time I knew the unbearable truth. Big Red took me to the medical clinic where I'd been two years prior. I knew why I was there and what I was there for. For two days I continued to bleed profusely, and on the third day I was taken to a different clinic. Once again I was given ether while my legs were put in those cold metal stirrups. This time when wakened I felt horrible both mentally and physically. My insides felt like they had a million stitches, and it was uncomfortable to walk or sit down because the doctor tightly sutured my cervix.

Big Red was angry again, almost as though she thought it was my fault, and she instructed me that no one was to know about this. Then she said the strangest thing: "But the one good thing from all this mess is you will probably never be able to have children." The subject of this whole "mess" having been caused by her perverted son, my father, never entered the picture, certainly not from her standpoint, as it was never discussed.

SLIMED ON

Blame, indescribable fear, and a sense of being covered with horrible slime enveloped me with a blanket of shame, and it continued to haunt me every day afterward. Guilt and shame became constant companions to my already grieving and broken heart. At the time I was only thirteen, but already a sex object used and abused by my own father. It was more than I could bear.

The thought of these immoral acts tormented me. If only I could awaken in a different place and all of this could just be a horrible nightmare. But it wasn't just a nightmare. I didn't know the word *incest* at the time, but that's what it was, horrendously and inconceivably depraved; it was a distasteful and unwanted reality to me. All of this was going on in my life at an age when most parents were preparing their precious daughters for entry into exciting teen years. But it was not to be true for me, and now I knew what it felt like to be even less than a soiled Kleenex, used and discarded in the trash.

While I didn't fully comprehend the magnitude of what had happened, however, I did believe I'd done something really bad, and that I must be a bad person. But Big Red most assuredly knew the reason for this abortion procedure! In 1938, she'd helped found Planned Parenthood in Fort Worth. Though abortions were illegal then, some Planned Parenthood clinics were used as cover-ups and as "alternatives" to unplanned pregnancies.

Much later, in 1988, Planned Parenthood celebrated its fiftieth anniversary in Fort Worth. Big Red had passed away by then, but someone from Planned Parenthood called and asked me to attend a banquet and to accept a memorial in honor of my grandmother.

The woman was stunned when I abruptly said, "No! I will not come to the Planned Parenthood dinner nor accept anything from you on behalf of my grandmother. I don't believe in your policies."

Planned Parenthood still holds bad memories in my mind. I never wanted to go back to that place, ever again. Those were frightening and traumatic experiences, physically, emotionally, and otherwise. It was impossible at the time for me to put these things in any sort of meaningful perspective, much less understand them.

CHAPTER 18

SILENCE THE PAIN

Money and power were wrecking my body, mind and spirit.
Surely suicide would silence the pain. . .

Life had become almost unbearable for me after the second horrible abortion experience during the eighth grade in early spring 1962. Abortions weren't legal at the time, but in plentiful supply for the wealthy, along with no questions asked. Abundant power and money were the things my family had; however, that money and power were wrecking my body, mind, and spirit. And sadly, I was soon to become a wrecking ball myself!

Following these life-shattering incidents, school ended and summer arrived, along with deep depression. Now I didn't want to go out and be with friends, and most days I spent sleeping. When not sleeping, I smoked endlessly. It was the only way I had at the time to endure the pain of the present.

SUICIDE ATTEMPT

All I could see was more of the same day after day. It was incest, but I'm not sure I would have known the word. I did know I felt starved for love and acceptance. My body and heart ached for loving arms to protect and shield me from The Shadow. Inside I was still just a little girl. Oh, how I wished I could dispose of this outward womanly body. I was confused and there seemed to be nothing to look forward to in life. The unrelenting feelings of being unwanted tormented my soul. Weary to my bones, the uselessness of my life loomed before me as a never-ending chain of oppression. I didn't have any answers to my questions, but I did wonder if these events had something to do with my being a bad person. The shame of being used again and again for things so degrading, coupled with not understanding the reasons behind these distasteful acts, ultimately pushed me to the edge of darkness.

Finally, thoughts of suicide overtook me and I was determined to end it all and take the fall into the chasm of nothingness. This seemed to be the only way to stop the endless pain, guilt, shame, and that sense of failure that continually plagued me. Ending my life at this point seemed to be the only viable answer.

Planning ahead, I didn't want Rosetta to be the one to find me, and so I picked a Wednesday because she had Thursdays off from work. Now I felt a strange excitement as I picked the outfit I would wear. I spent all of Wednesday afternoon fixing my hair and doing my nails. I wanted to look perfect lying in bed when Mother found me the next morning. I knew Mother would be the one to come in to wake me up because it was July, with early sunrises. Mother hated for me to sleep past noon, so she would bring a metal pan into my room and continually hit it with a spoon to get me up. I relished the thought that she'd be shocked to discover Father's Sleeping Beauty permanently still and finally at rest; but it would be too late, and no one would be able to break the spell of the wicked witch this time.

Around 11:30 that evening, after getting dressed, coiffed, and looking the way I knew my mother would approve, I swallowed the codeine and aspirin taken from my parents' medicine cabinet. After taking twelve pills, I put the fifty-plus remaining tablets in water to dissolve and gulped down the deadly concoction. Then I called one of my close friends and said good-bye. I laid down on the bed, hands crossed, doing my best to resemble Sleeping Beauty or Snow White, closed my eyes, and hoped to wake up somewhere over the rainbow. Surely suicide would silence the pain I felt inside.

It didn't take long and the room started to spin; I became clammy and sweaty, warm and feverish. I jumped up, pulled the headband out of my hair, ripped off my clothes, and went into the bathroom to throw up. I'd heard raw eggs help you throw up, so I made my way to the kitchen and got an egg, but I couldn't bring myself to swallow it. My stomach was now bloated, and my head was pounding and throbbing with the pain I was so hoping to get rid of. I lay down on the bathroom floor and moaned. This was turning out to be an awful experience. Now I didn't know if I wanted to die from feeling so horrible or because I hated my life. But this had turned into a miserable, pain-filled exercise in futility.

RESCUE

Faintly, I heard a ringing telephone in the background. My friend had talked her older brother into calling my parents, and he told them they needed to check on me. The door to my bedroom burst open, and Mother found me lying on the floor. "Oh, for God's sake, Carmyn, what have you done?"

She left quickly, and the next thing I remember is being picked up by Father, put in the car, and rushed to the emergency room. During the brief trip to the hospital, Father held me in the back seat, screaming, "Don't die. Oh God, please don't let her die." (It's a wonder we made it to the hospital; my mother, who seldom drove, was behind the wheel.)

I vaguely remember Father running down the hallway at the hospital screaming for someone to help. Father, who had taken my innocence away, was now trying to save me. Irony of ironies!

HOSPITALIZATION

Orderlies placed me on a stretcher, and I was rushed to a room where they stuck a tube down my nose into my stomach. Everything was becoming blurred and seemed far away. But I heard the doctors ask: "How many pills did you take? What did you take?" Then I was in darkness.

The next day I awoke and was alone in a hospital room. IVs were hanging everywhere, and I knew I was still alive. The nurses continued to monitor my blood pressure; I pretended to be asleep so I wouldn't have to answer any questions.

Mother came to the hospital once during the five days I was there, and Father never did come. The day Mother came she stormed into my hospital room and first thing out of her mouth was, "How could you do this to us?" I closed my eyes and fought back my tears, *Can't believe I did this to them? Doesn't anybody see what is being done to me? ! I desperately wanted to scream out loud!* She said Brother asked if I was still alive. She told him yes and said that he went on to say, "It's a shame she didn't die. She's so miserable." Those words felt like salt poured into my broken, wounded heart. He was right; I should have died. No one wanted me.

Mother told me I couldn't do anything right but make a mess of things, and I guessed that included my unsuccessful attempt at suicide. She left, and no one came to see me in the hospital after that. Four days later, I was ready to leave the hospital. The doctors and nurses never asked questions about the whys of what had happened. It was as if I had food poisoning—an inconvenient and expensive bout of some everyday illness. This sorry episode reinforced my belief that I mattered to no one.

Reminder and Silence

Willie D was sent to pick me up. He brought some clean clothes for me to wear home, but as I opened the small bag, my heart almost stopped! Mother had malevolently sent the outfit I wore when trying to commit suicide, complete with the headband. Mother always made it a point to pull my hair off my face as she pointedly reminded me what a mop I looked like to her. That is why I took such great effort to look like a fictional fairy-tale character the night I tried to end my life. I was hoping to be a cold, still reminder of her obsession with her idols of perfection. Numbly, I dressed myself in defeat. Willie D waited outside to drive me home.

When I arrived home, it was time for dinner. My parents were at their usual places and Brother, as usual, was gone. No one said a word. As I took my place at the table, we all acted like nothing had ever happened. It was strange not to acknowledge this tragic event marking my sordid and meaningless existence. It felt like I wasn't even in the room.

This event was never brought up by the adult side of my existence again. But there was a significant side benefit: The Shadow never again returned to my room. There would have been too many unanswerable questions and perhaps, even worse, someone might be forced to acknowledge a serious problem existed . . . with me? After all, why would a normal, well-adjusted thirteen-year-old girl who had every material advantage try to take her own life? The Shadow knew! Mother and my grandparents knew! And so did I.

FAMILY SECRETS

This family secret was held in darkness for a long time. Three years later, at age sixteen, I slit my wrist, once again crying out for help. Mother rationalized this embarrassing incident by saying it was over a boy I was dating.

Once again, I was crying out for help, but no one seemed to notice or care. Such was life in my dreary world of apparent non-existence. I was labeled as the overly emotional and unstable misfit of the family. This only reinforced the hurtful belief that there was something terribly wrong with me. Everyone and everything else in my life appeared regular and normal, at least from all outward appearances. I surmised that I was the only irregular one in our small world on the privileged side of town.

CHAPTER 19

LET THE GAMES BEGIN

My magnetic compass for trouble continued unabated.

Three weeks after returning home from the hospital, I told Mother that I wanted to go to a boarding school. Mother had gone to Hockaday, in Dallas, and I had decided that would be best for me too. She was thrilled, not that I was doing what she had done, but that I would be gone and out of her house.

Two weeks later, I drove Mother and myself to Dallas to take the entrance exam and see the school. After viewing the school, which had been rebuilt in a different location since Mother was there, I got excited about going away. Maybe this would be my new chance in life.

I was entering the ninth grade, which in 1963 was junior high school. Fort Worth high schools were conducted for the tenth through twelfth grades, but Hockaday considered the ninth grade a part of high school, so it felt really cool to say I was attending high school at age fourteen.

New Wardrobe

Two weeks later, Hockaday called and said I'd been accepted. Mother went into high gear, buying all the right clothes for me, even though the school required us to wear uniforms to class. The uniforms were a hunter green, pleated skirt and an ivory blazer with hunter green trim and the Hockaday logo. The required shoes were brown-and-white saddle oxfords. I would need Sunday attire for church and various outfits for cultural outings.

Mother was a genius at finding the right person to coordinate my personal wardrobe. Everything from lingerie to purses and hats was all taken care of. No cost was to be spared in getting me out of the house, and for all practical purposes, out of their everyday lives. How convenient, this one-size solution seemed to fit all concerned.

Pranks and Detention

At Hockaday, my magnetic compass for trouble continued unabated. My studies were going reasonably well, and I really enjoyed the school's educational program. I met and enjoyed knowing several interesting girls from all parts of the United States. Some were boarders like me, and some were day students who attended school only during the day since they lived in Dallas. During my first year of high school, I had wonderful opportunities to go to the homes of these new friends. Occasionally I still hear from them, and we sometimes get together at reunions.

Continuing my predisposition for trouble, I was frequently in detention for some prank. As boarders, we dressed for bed and then went to study hall in the activity room. The juniors and seniors could study in their rooms if they had good grades, but I didn't qualify for that perk. If one was in detention, she stayed dressed in uniform and went to the school library for study hall each evening.

Even though I was in detention, I still discovered ways to rebel and get in trouble. One evening while in the library, my roommate and I set half a dozen alarm clocks to go off ten minutes apart. We hid the clocks behind the bookshelves with eager anticipation, and I nearly wet my pants from laughing so hard watching the librarian trying to locate all the alarms. Needless to say, more detention followed. At the time it seemed worth it to have so thoroughly enjoyed the pranks and the bewilderment of the school librarian.

REPUTATION AND LEAVING

No matter what happened or how perfect the plan for the prank seemed to be, we got in trouble every time, which, for the most part, was certainly well deserved. But one day a girl down the hall had a hundred dollars stolen from the purse in her room. Being a known troublemaker, I was immediately blamed! While I'd done a lot of foolish things at Hockaday, stealing from others was not one of them.

It hurt to know that I was considered a thief, and this changed things at school for me. My reputation for pranks had apparently permanently stained my reputation, and I was deemed presumptively guilty of every bad occurrence.

Finally, in March of the second semester, I called Father at five one morning and told him that if he didn't come get me, I was going to tell everybody what he had done to me. By nine, one of the Company drivers arrived, loaded up my things, and I was gone.

Funny, in an odd sort of way, how one's life can change so quickly.

CHAPTER 20

WHAT A LIFE!

New freedoms surfaced . . . I ruled

I returned home from Hockaday with a new realization that I could use my silence as a form of blackmail against Father. I ruled. He knew it, and I knew it. This nearly destroyed both of us in the end. My blame and his guilt resulted in many hurtful choices, all of which resulted in self-destructive behavioral patterns for both of us.

By now, Mother had started drinking again and Father's health was declining from his excessive alcohol intake and unfiltered cigarettes. While I was away at Hockaday for a semester and a half, Father had lost between sixty to eighty pounds. He had always been considerably overweight, and that, combined with his heavy drinking and poor eating habits, had resulted in the onset of diabetes. Previously, Father had been bigger than life and was extremely powerful in my mind, but now he looked old, beaten down by life, and weak. He was only in his forties, but looked seventy.

NEW FREEDOM, PAYBACK

New freedoms surfaced with my newfound control over Father. The suicide attempt had ironically turned the cards in my direction, and now I was the one in charge. Of course, Mother resented that I got away with spending as much money as I wanted. Both parents constantly bickered over Mother's excessive spending, but nothing was ever said or done about mine. This created considerable friction and tension in their marriage and, predictably, more resentment from Mother toward me. I could not have cared less. As far as I was concerned, they were both getting payback. In a perverse sort of way, that felt good, and now I was really into feeling good. It had been a long time getting there.

Now I could buy or get anything as long as I kept my silence. It was great! At age fourteen I had a car of my own, an unlimited checking account, charge accounts at all the fine department stores, and access to any material pleasure I wanted. Father purchased Dallas Cowboys football tickets at the Cotton Bowl, hockey tickets, Golden Gloves tickets or entrances to any "happening" type of event in Fort Worth. Father would get me tickets to all of these events, and they were heady experiences for a young teenager.

In March of 1964, I had transferred from Hockaday to a private school in Fort Worth. The classes were smaller; the ninth grade consisted of only twenty or thirty students. Most of the kids had attended different elementary and junior high schools than me, so it was exciting and fun to meet new students my own age. Even better, no one was familiar with my background.

WORK AFTER SCHOOL

By the time the eleventh grade arrived, I had transferred to a public high school. The Fort Worth public school system had a co-op program in which you were able to be dismissed at 1 pm and then work at a job for school credit. During those last two years of high school while working at Father's plant, I managed to put in enough school hours per week typing W-2 forms, logging shipping information, paying company expenses, and working in the lab to test the content of the product we produced.

It was fun working for a paycheck, and I enjoyed working with the other company employees. My favorite job was to work the telephone switchboard, and at Christmas I'd plug in all the office phones in my area and ring "Jingle Bells" on the desk phones. Of course Father, the boss, would be out to lunch!

I never worked on Fridays—most Friday mornings I'd get an early dismissal from school. At the beginning of each school year I wrote a dismissal excuse for myself on Mother's monogrammed note cards. The school kept her writing on record to verify notes, but it was always my signature, so they never knew, and I had no problems getting dismissed from school whenever I wanted.

WEEKENDS AWAY

When leaving home for the weekend, I would usually tell Rosetta that I was spending the night with a friend. The next day I'd call and tell Rosetta or Mother I was spending another night away. Cell phones and car phones had not been invented yet, so it was difficult to trace where I actually was. I'd leave a friend's private phone number just in case Mother might call, but not once did she ever try to get in touch or locate me.

Both parents were usually drunk on the weekends, especially at night, so I don't think they even thought of my whereabouts. Literally, I could tell Mother that I was going to be here or there, and she never questioned my actions or the events. Both parents thought it important for me to be able to hold my liquor, so I was allowed to drink at home beginning at fourteen years of age. Father had a large liquor closet, and I was permitted to take whatever I wanted from scotch, vodka, rum, and beer. They also allowed me to smoke freely at home. Mother had cigarette urns with matching lighters and Lalique crystal ashtrays on the tables even in my bedroom. She made sure they were always full too! Permissiveness ran rampant at my parents' house.

MOTEL LIFE

Looking back, I marvel that I survived the years from 1963 to 1967.

There were three motels around town where I usually checked in for the weekend. I attended parties or sporting events and then went back to the motel to sleep. There I watched TV, played solitaire, and smoked. On several occasions I drove to Austin and stayed by myself at the Hyatt Hotel on Austin's Town Lake to attend UT (University of Texas) fraternity parties.

Since I looked much older than my real age, it was easy to walk into any liquor store and buy alcohol without being asked for ID. Many times I ate alone at Cattleman's Steak House or went to a movie downtown. It didn't bother me to do things on my own. In fact, I enjoyed being away from home and doing things alone. It seemed the norm to me.

Since I was used to being alone, I preferred to be alone in some motel rather than alone at home. Actually, it was great, because I didn't have to be around my parents, their drinking, their arguing, and all the negativity that permeated our house. My home surroundings were just not appealing, even in the luxury of Mother's perfectly kept house. And so, the peaceful surroundings at the Green Oaks Inn were worth it all.

DEGRADING RELATIONSHIP

Unfortunately, by this time in my life I began having an affair with a man six years older than myself. Looking back on this strange bedfellow arrangement, I now realize it was something of a lifesaver at the time. Each weekend I'd take off for the hinterlands so I wouldn't have to be at home, and I was glad to have his company on many occasions. But it's difficult to look back on this abnormal relationship, particularly now that I have teenage grandchildren. The word *unhealthy* captures the reality, but of course I was unaware what "healthy" and "normal" dating relationships actually were.

What a degrading and heartrending lifestyle for a teenager to be trapped in. Obviously, this is not how those precious adolescent years should be spent. How thankful I am today that the HIV virus and other sexually transmitted diseases were not prevalent during those teen years of badly chosen behavior. Most of my life up until then had felt so lonely that these secret times with him felt good and like someone really cared for me. I was looking for love in all the wrong places, and the fruit was rotten and stained.

Never having known what a healthy relationship was, I failed to understand that this dating routine was just a different form of The Shadow. By then, I was accustomed to being exploited and used as a commodity, but was so desperate for love it didn't seem to matter.

CHAPTER 21

AHOY MATE!

*I learned four-letter words I'd never known before,
words like* work, wash, *and* care, *and I learned
that if I didn't do these things, no one else would!
The boat was a wonderful refuge for an adrift teen.*

When I turned fourteen in the summer of 1963, I learned to water ski. I really enjoyed waterskiing and especially loved the nearby Eagle Mountain Lake blue-green waters. On my fifteenth birthday, in 1964, the grandparents handed me the keys to a genuine burnished, high-gloss, wood classic, Chris-Craft inboard/outboard ski boat. Predictably, neither Mother nor my grandparents ever took time to see that watercraft or me enjoying it. Father saw it once, and even then, it was merely a fleeting look.

Grandfather told me to go to Marion Herring's boat harbor on Eagle Mountain Lake and ask which slip my new boat was stored in. I'd never driven a ski boat in my life. (Maybe the grandparents wanted to see how quickly I could crash and end up wrecked on the Eagle Mountain Lake Dam? Can you imagine a high-powered ski boat at the hands of an inexperienced fifteen-year-old?) Although my birthday was not until June 16, the grandparents gave me that ski boat early in the spring of 1965 so that I was able to enjoy the use of that gorgeous watercraft for the entire summer.

One Saturday morning I called my friend who lived across the street and asked her to go with me to see this new pleasure-craft. We drove thirty minutes to the lake, and one of the storekeepers at the Marina showed me the brand new Chris-Craft. It was absolutely beautiful, navy and white, with a high-gloss hardwood bow, stern, and sides. This new acquisition was definitely a real delight and worthy of being thankful for. My grandparents' ranch brand was displayed largely on the stern of the boat. I guess it was important for everyone on Eagle Mountain Lake to know who purchased this expensive Chris-Craft.

Because I was afraid to try and maneuver the boat out of the boat stall, my friend and I pushed it out of the stall using our hands. When I turned the ignition key, the boat's powerful engine revved! Here we go! The wind was blowing gustily that day, and there were flag warnings on area lakes. However, being a novice, I was totally unaware what those meant. Once we left the slough and hit open water, the white-capped waves began buffeting the sides of the boat and washing over the sides. No wonder there weren't any other boats on the water that day. Duh!

We bounced around all over the lake on the choppy, wind-driven, whitecap waters. Finally, after only a short while, better judgment prompted me to head back to the marina. A fresh new problem was then presented. How in the world was I going to maneuver this ungainly twenty-foot-long boat back into that tiny boat slip? Just as we had embarked, so we got it back in, simply by turning the engine off and paddling the craft back into its assigned stall. I felt somewhat victorious over nature and my own inexperience at handling this watercraft.

LESSONS FROM A TRUE FRIEND

Gilmore, a friend who lived at the lake, upon learning of my lack of boating skills, took pity. He took it upon himself that summer to teach me how to pilot my boat, and thankfully, I learned the boating equivalent of the "rules of the road." Gilmore was an expert watercraft navigator since his father had a large cabin-cruiser on the lake. Gilmore had grown up around boats, skiing, and Eagle Mountain Lake for most of his life.

He taught me to take pride and responsibility for the maintenance and care of my new boat that summer. He taught me four-letter words I'd never heard before, words like *work, wash,* and *take care,* and I learned that if I didn't do these things, no one else would.

Sometimes I went to the lake and drove the pleasure boat around by myself. I relished the quietness and serene beauty of the lake and its tree-lined shores. It was a wonderful refuge for an adrift teen. That Chris-Craft boat was a great learning experience for me in my young life, coming at an age when I was desperately in need of good guidance.

Hawaii Beckons

In the summer of 1966 I went to summer school in Hawaii. It was the most wonderful summer of my young life there on those warm Pacific shores. I was at last free to be me, and that felt good. It was a heartening new experience and one that expanded my sense of well-being. In Hawaii I was free to be and free from the stigma of my family name. For once in my life I didn't have to be anxious about how I looked, or how I spoke, or how I did things. After my morning classes in school it was time to surf, hang out on the beach, and meet some fun, amazing, and truly wonderful young people from all over the United States. I attended concerts at the Hawaiian Hall where I saw Elvis, the Rolling Stones, the Yardbirds, and Otis Redding. What a blast! It was literally heaven on earth.

Thankfully, the boys I met were not interested in serious relationships . . . we were just friends trying to sort through our lives and find the pathways most suitable for us. That summer I gained renewed strength to return to Fort Worth and finish high school with a plan to return and attend the University of Hawaii.

Return to the Familiar

Unfortunately, those feelings of well-being soon fell by the wayside almost as soon as my feet touched the mainland. I began dating another man seven years older; we had a lot in common—skiing, horseback riding, hunting, and rock music. We went out almost every night and my parents didn't know what to think of my long-haired boyfriend.

CHAPTER 22

MY COMING OUT

It was embarrassing for me, and initially uncomfortable.

My parents were shocked when I became engaged at age seventeen, telling them we had agreed to wait a year before we got married. So Mother called her priest and asked if there was anything she could do to stop the proposed marriage. The Episcopalian priest told her not to let me know she was upset because I might run off and elope. He said to go along with the plans and maybe, over time, I'd realize this was not the right thing to do. Truthfully, the only reason I wanted to get married was to leave home and run away from all the madness of my parents' drinking and destructive lifestyles, not to mention my own downward slide.

TIME FOR A DEBUT

When Father's parents found out I was getting married, Grandfather almost had a stroke. He had waited his whole life to see his only granddaughter make her formal debut into Fort Worth's elite society. He was adamant I was not going to miss mine. It seemed to me somewhat akin to raising a fine broodmare and then reaping the acclaim of having done so. Anyway, I knew instinctively it wasn't because he was proud of me. It was just another marker of his financial, social, and business successes.

The proper age for a young woman in polite society to make her debut is usually age twenty, after finishing her sophomore year in college. But since I was turning eighteen in three weeks, Grandfather pulled a few strings and I was allowed to make my debut early. Most assuredly, I didn't want to do this. It seemed hypocritical, to say the least. My fiancé was really upset and wanted me to promise I wouldn't agree to make my debut. He was afraid I might realize the fun and glamour of the social scene and then decide not to get married. Never having felt comfortable in these types of social settings, I decided not to attend the deb parties and do all the things debutantes are supposed to do. But as was always the case, Grandfather won out on the making-my-debut issue.

In 1967 there were twenty-three debutantes to be presented at two separate balls. Our first meeting with the social hierarchy for the coming party season for Fort Worth society was the day after my eighteenth birthday in June of that year. A welcoming cocktail party for all the young women and their parents was held at The Club. The purpose of this social was to introduce the debutantes and go over the details of the coming deb season, which culminated with the debs' grand and extravagant presentations at two separate galas.

UNEASY

Most of the debs were my brother's age; that is, two years older, and had attended high school with him. I felt like a fool, as I knew none of them. It was embarrassing and initially uncomfortable for me. I wondered what they thought about me, breaking the normal social rules to make my debut at an early age. To my surprise, they could not have been nicer, and they accepted me right away, thank goodness. Several of those girls became my dearest and closest friends through sharing the debut experience. To this day, forty-plus years after our debuts, we continue to meet once a month for lunch. I really cherish their friendships.

The social director passed out a sheet of paper with a list of parties and the dates of the various events planned for the 1967 debutante season. There were ninety-eight parties total, ranging from teas to cocktail parties before large balls, honoring particular debutantes and their families. The list seemed endless! Intuitively, I knew why I didn't want to go through this discomforting ordeal! This deb scene was just another socially elite realm where I didn't fit

COMING OUT

My upcoming debut was a big event around our house, and it was called a "coming out" party. (Nowadays that term means something totally different, so you never hear that expression used for debutantes today!) It seemed to me that my debut was like a "show and tell" for my parents and, especially, Grandfather. He gave me two mink coats, diamond bracelets, necklaces, earrings, other jewels, and also a new Buick Riviera. Big Red took me to Dallas, and I was showered with a wardrobe of couture clothes from Neiman Marcus. A personal wardrobe consultant put showcase outfits together for each of the debutante parties. This certainly wasn't done for my enjoyment; it was promoted to showcase Grandfather, his wealth, social prominence, and business successes.

The whole coming-out process was a fabricated debacle for me, and its pretentious showiness made me ill. It seemed Grandfather was trying to put me on an auction block, and the bachelor-bidders could come and offer their best bid-price. The eying of me from head to toe also felt like critical judgments from the "fashion police" matrons of society and women in general. Even worse, many of the men's cold stares were just as creepy as The Shadow's had been in my earlier teenage years. I hated being in the spotlight with my every movement being gawked at by the society judges. Even though engaged, my grandparents were hopeful I'd break my engagement and end up marrying someone more socially acceptable in their eyes. What a person had and did for a living wasn't on my list of requirements for a potential mate. Truthfully, I didn't know what was on my spousal qualifications list. I just knew that I wanted out of where I was.

Big Red had told me to never marry a man for love. "Love dies!" she said. "However, if you marry a man for his money, you will always be happy." I guess she thought that worked for her, but the harsh reality of their horrendous relationship denied the sad truth with their continuing unresolved conflict. Frankly, I didn't trust a man with money. The men I knew were not to be trusted with anything of value, especially me.

All I really wanted was to be loved and respected, and more importantly, to be a significant part of someone's life—someone I could love, admire, and respect in return. Starved for love and affection, I thought I knew where to find it. But I was so wrong and so naïve.

WEDDING BELLS

After my debut presentation in the fall of 1967, the date was set for a wedding, which was to be held in April 1968. However, I began to have second thoughts, as my fiancé and I argued constantly over many things, and he didn't trust me either. He was easily jealous and questioned my every move, whether I was with him or not. Then I found out he had been lying for months about his whereabouts and what he was doing. For months he'd told me that he was at gambling establishments at nights betting on football games. The truth was that those games had stopped several months before, and he just didn't want me to know where he was, nor what was taking place. Now I didn't need any excuse to be convinced my intuition was correct.

Immediately I called off the wedding and left with a friend of mine to go out of town and get away.

The two of us went to charming Salado, Texas to stay at the Stage-coach Inn and shop among the heralded antique shops and art galleries. But two hours later, Father called and said my ex-fiancé's mother had died. He said I needed to come back for her funeral. Not wanting to feel guilty over this, I returned home to attend the funeral.

On the ride back to Fort Worth I told my friend, "I will go to the funeral, but I am not going to marry him." On this decision not to marry, I was determined to stand my ground!

CHAPTER 23

MAKE-BELIEVE

I hadn't learned to trust my own instincts . . .
I hadn't developed the inner strength to stand up for myself
with the confidence to do what I desired rather than give
in to the feelings of others.

My ex-fiancé was distraught over his mother's death, his sense of loss having been accentuated due to his parents having been divorced for more than seventeen years. "I don't have anyone, and besides, my mother was counting on us to marry," he said as he begged me to reconsider.

Finally, feeling sorry for his plight, I gave in and agreed to get married, even though my heart said no. I hadn't yet learned to trust my own instincts concerning love and marriage. I hadn't developed the inner strength to stand up for myself and have the confidence to do what I desired rather than give into the feelings of others.

FAIRY TALE WEDDING

The wedding came and was beautiful in its presentation. Over twelve hundred invitations were sent, and I received splendid wedding gifts, which filled three rooms in my parents' house. Mother, with the help of professional wedding coordinators, made sure every detail was properly attended to, and the end result was a high-fashion extravaganza.

As a young child, during the times spent in the field of daisies at the Ranch, I'd dreamed and fantasized about my castle-in-the-sky wedding one day. Thus, I already knew how I wanted it to be presented. My bridesmaids wore pale yellow dresses with big yellow hats, just like the one Grace Kelly wore in the movie *High Society*. To my delight, I'd been able to find the perfect chiffon dresses and had the bridesmaids' hats custom-made out of a beautiful yellow tulle. My bridal gown had daisies cut in the lace of the gown, and I wore exquisite lace, high heeled shoes. The bridesmaids carried little woven baskets filled with daisies. And fresh yellow-centered daisies were everywhere—on the white linen tablecloth tables filling the reception area held at The Club, along with tons of white lilies, gladiolas, and white hydrangeas. It was my little girl's fantasy come true, but this marriage was not make-believe. It became a harsh and combative relational reality soon enough.

On the day of the April wedding, there was a beautiful brunch at one of the Country Clubs for more than three hundred out-of-town guests. My next door neighbor was a bridesmaid, and she picked me up to ride to The Club for the morning brunch. Within ten minutes after arriving, I suddenly felt nauseated and sick. So I excused myself and went to the ladies room. My face was clammy and I started throwing up. Margaret found me in the bathroom, and she left to tell Mother she was taking me home. Margaret had to pull the car over twice on the way home for me to throw up. Once at home, I continued to be sick until, finally, I got the dry heaves. The smells and feelings of nausea were even worse as I couldn't seem to shake this sense of impending doom.

Mother returned home and called our family doctor. He came to the house and gave me a shot—of what, I know not. Mother woke me at 5 PM to go to St. John's Episcopal Church to get ready for my wedding. Thankfully, I was slightly drugged throughout the whole wedding ceremony and reception and didn't feel the nausea again. Vividly,

I do remember walking down the aisle with Father and desperately thinking of ways to try and get out of this upcoming disaster. I wanted to bolt and run away through the side door of the church, but I was too chicken to brave up and do what was best for me.

MARITAL REALITY

The marriage was hard for me, but it didn't seem to bother my pretend-groom any. Now I was going to school, working, and keeping a house. My marriage seemed more like that of being a mother than being a wife. Having recently lost his mother, I was awarded her place, but sadly, it was in the context of our hopeless marriage. My new roommate regularly went off to the pool hall and stayed late each night. He didn't have a job, so Father employed him in our family oil company. He was required to visit the oil well drill sites and was gone from our home three or four days at a time. Unknown to me at the time, he was also taking his friends and other girls with him.

The harsh reality of an unwanted marriage began to sink in as I realized this was not the same man I thought I'd known before we got married. No longer was he interested in horses and hunting or doing fun things with me. The only thing we had in common was water-skiing, and since that was only a summer sport we rarely spent time with each other. The drudgery of this awful marriage was such that each of us did our own thing. Although living in the same house, we no longer shared the same bed. It had been almost a year since we had been intimate with one another, and I was thankful that marital duty was no longer required.

ANTIQUE UNCLE

During the summer of 1969, we visited my mother's brother, who lived in San Francisco. He owned an antique store and traveled all over Europe buying antiques, as well as having business connections in New York.

My uncle loved to have cocktail drinks in the evenings, but his feel-good tendencies went beyond that and later turned into an addiction to narcotics. It seemed like he seldom slept, and he would roam his San Francisco flat all hours of the night. He was always funny and shared the same dry wit as Mother. I'd been aware that something had happened between Mother and her brother when she was twelve and he was fourteen, but didn't know the full story.

IIn San Francisco, the three of us—actually the two of them—would visit into the wee hours of the night talking about how we needed to move away from Fort Worth. The day before we returned from San Francisco, in July 1969, we sat on the deck of a quaint harbor-front restaurant in Sausalito overlooking the San Francisco Bay and had drinks with my uncle. The two of them were engrossed in deep conversation, so I left the table and went to sit on a bench by the bay. I watched the sailboats glide across the sparkling blue ocean waters and in that translucent moment, I promised myself that after leaving San Francisco, I'd start over to make a different life away from my family. Once again, I wanted out, but now I was both determined and committed, come what might.

In 1971 my uncle drove his sports car off the winding roads in the Napa Valley of Northern California and died in a solo car crash. In 1997, I was told by his oldest son that he had confessed to raping his sister, my mother, when she was twelve. (My mother never spoke about this to me.)

DIVORCE OUT

My uncle was correct. We did need to move from Fort Worth, but regarding this issue, what I'd decided on was only about me. My pretend-husband was not included, and it was time for a change, a radical change. Somehow, I needed to find a way out of this marriage. I didn't know how to explain to him that I wanted a divorce, but knew I had to find the courage. Stifled and smothered in this suffocatingly dead relationship, I was certain it would never work.

That was the final push I needed, and so I left and filed for divorce. He tried to keep the marriage together, but actually it had ended before it began. I was now twenty years old, and so I returned back home to live with my parents.

I soon left for New Orleans with a friend to get away from all the mess I had been experiencing in Fort Worth.

CHAPTER 24

CLARK KENT APPEARS

I knew intuitively that I'd just met my Superman . . .
I was certain he was the one for me.

Upon returning from New Orleans, I was depressed, and yet determined to make a new life for myself. A workout program was begun and I attempted to jog, but I walked more, since I was a habitual smoker by this time.

Occasionally, I modeled for different department stores in Fort Worth, with times at Neiman Marcus in the Zodiac Room in Dallas, as well as other style shows in Fort Worth. By now, depression, along with smoking, suppressed my appetite enough that eating became secondary. I lost weight easily and quickly, and being five-foot-ten and weighing 118 pounds, I obsessed about getting down to 112 and into a size 4 or 6 dress.

My uncle knew I wanted to be a model, and with his connections in New York, he could help get my foot in the door of the fashion world.

With a modeling career I could get on the road to success and fashion fame. Twiggy had just hit the fashion model magazines, and super skinny was in. Now I weighed 113, and by the time I'd leave for New York, 108 seemed easily attainable. It seemed a much better modeling weight for me with my height.

While in Fort Worth, I stayed in my room at home going through every fashion magazine that could be found. I dreamed of being a model and fantasized that I was a supermodel appearing on the cover of *Vogue*. I'd show the world, especially those in my family and Fort Worth, how valuable I was. Although these mental excursions were just fantasies, they kept me going and kept me from giving up on life and myself.

THE RODEO

Then one evening there came a knock on my bedroom door. I opened it and there was Brother. We hadn't seen or spent much time with each other since I'd gotten married and then separated. Brother never cared for my soon-to-be ex-husband, so we had drifted apart. But here he was now, and I was so glad to see him.

Brother said, "Enough of this. Get dressed. I'm taking you to the rodeo."

As was customary for me, I immediately started the process of getting myself together. Quickly I put on my makeup, lined my brown eyes with black eyeliner, tossed my long, dark hair back, and then let it hang loosely about my shoulders. I dressed in a camel hair miniskirt, brown cashmere turtleneck sweater, and matching camel hair jacket with calf-length brown suede boots coming up over my knees. Yes, this was the exact look I wanted. A touch of Shalimar perfume and I was ready to go.

The Fort Worth Stock Show and Rodeo was an annual event which our family members faithfully attended every year in early January. Grandfather was chairman of the Stock Show, so this was indeed a big thing in our ranching family.

BACKSTAGE CLUB

We went to Will Rogers Coliseum to watch some of the indoor rodeo and then headed up to the Backstage Club. Around 10:30 PM we decided it was time to go home and got off the elevator on the ground level just as a friend of Brother's was about to step on. He proceeded to convince the two of us to head back upstairs for another drink.

We followed him to a table, and as we walked over I glanced up and saw a handsome man watching me walk across the room. Suddenly, it was as if everything was in slow motion with each step I took. Dressed in a suit and tie, he had dark hair and looked professional. He was definitely conservative, not the kind of man I had ever been out with before. Until then, most men I'd dated wore long hair and were total clothes horses wearing all the latest fads. This man was wearing a pair of black-rimmed glasses and was slowly taking them off to put in his coat pocket. Our eyes locked together, and he didn't take his eyes off of me. My eyes were drawn to his sparkling blue eyes, and for a moment, time seemed to stand still. By the time I reached his table, he stood up and said, "I'm Hal Sparks."

I smiled, and Brother reached his hand out to shake Hal's and said, "Hal, this is my sister, Carmyn," as he proudly introduced me. Even Brother seemed to enjoy showing his good-looking sister off.

This handsome young man pulled a chair out for me to sit down. Everyone else in the room disappeared from view as Hal and I began talking. Hal and Brother were officers together in a men's social club.

A DATE WITH CLARK KENT

The Backstage Club was displaying various works of art for its Cowtown patrons. Several pictures from a local art gallery lined the walls of the club for Western art lovers to view and perhaps purchase. After a drink, Hal asked me to walk around and look at the artwork displayed. As we viewed the various selections of art, he asked me to go to the TCU basketball game the next night. Without hesitation, "yes" came flying out of my mouth.

We went back to the table, and Brother asked Hal if he would take me home. I was mortified, but at least Hal had already asked me for a date. Brother had just met a cute, red-haired cowgirl and didn't want his little sister tagging along.

Hal and I drove back to my parents' house, but we made little conversation. I was a bit uncomfortable and I felt best to sit in silence rather than try to make small talk. I still didn't feel I had great social skills, even though Mother was the queen of nonstop chatter. I just felt it was smarter to say nothing if you had nothing of substance to say. Months later, Hal told me it was a quality he liked about me. I didn't realize it at the time, but he was sizing up my ability to feel comfortable with him without having to make a lot of conversation. Wasn't that funny—as in, unusual.

We walked to the door and said goodnight. He said he'd call the next day to set the time to pick me up for our date. My heart was leaping with anticipation.

I walked in the door to our house starry-eyed and immediately informed Mother, who was still up, that I'd just met the man I was going to marry. It had been six months since filing for divorce, and it was then about three weeks before becoming final. Mother sarcastically responded, "Can we get this divorce over first?"

Feeling excited, I glided to my room walking on a cloud. What was it about him? My subconscious knew. I'd met Clark Kent, and as he had taken off his dark-rimmed glasses to watch me walk across the Backstage Club, I knew intuitively that I'd just met my Superman. I can't say why or how, but I was certain he was the one for me.

CHAPTER 25

FRUITCAKE, ANYONE?

Hal must have thought, Who is this fruitcake I married!

My dreams of going to New York and having a modeling career never happened. Thankfully, January eighth, exactly one year after meeting my Superman, I married him. By now I was expecting a child and Mother was offended—and offensive—as well. Now understand that God will sometimes offend our minds in order to reveal our hearts so that we see and understand something about ourselves that formerly we did not. Mother's heart was revealed that day! She was mortified about her daughter's soon-to-be-known pregnant condition at the altar of marriage.

Upon learning of my pregnancy, I was shocked and thrilled at the same time, as I'd been told previously by Big Red and Mother that I could never have children. In all the years of sexual activity and my first marriage, I'd never taken any precautions. I thought I'd be barren for life.

Feeling different one day after Hal and I'd been dating awhile, I took a sample of my urine to be tested. This was long before the day of home pregnancy tests. I prayed I might be carrying Hal's child. God answered my prayer, and not only did he answer that prayer, but he gave me a daughter too. A beautiful little girl, Elizabeth, and when I first held her I told her that life was going to be wonderful, and I would always be there to love and take care of her.

FAMILY CONFLICTS

During our first years of marriage, the conflicts between Mother and my husband were endless and relentless, and the pressures from his family as well almost did us in. There were widely varying expectations from both sides of our two families. Our individual family traditions and different backgrounds led to many conflicts between the two of us. Each of us had brought a lot of excess baggage into our marriage. It was to take a long time of counseling and working through our issues before peace and harmony would set in.

In a matter of two years we had two children. During the first trimester of my second pregnancy, I got a virus and ran a 105-degree temperature. Not knowing I was pregnant, our family doctor ordered abdominal and bladder X-rays. I was put on heavy antibiotics, and three weeks later learned I was pregnant. I was elated and ecstatic at the same time. On my first visit to the OB-GYN, my balloon of joy burst when told there was only a 20 percent chance the baby would be normal due to the virus, not to mention the X-rays. Our doctor suggested an abortion. Decidedly no! This was not an option, not ever. When I left the doctor's office, I put the thought of an abortion completely out of my mind.

The next day our pediatrician called and suggested an abortion too. Hal was very concerned and had misgivings, but I never gave the matter a second thought. I knew I could never go through the horror of that awful experience again. Our baby was fine, and that was that. End of discussion.

SECOND DAUGHTER

Nine months later we had a beautiful baby girl, our second daughter, and I was thrilled and delighted. There was nothing wrong with her except that her legs were turned a little inward and the cartilage of her precious little ears was crushed, cresting to come to a slight point. She was beautiful and the happiest baby I'd ever seen, full of joy and a zest for life. Her eager, happy, smiling countenance was uplifting to our whole family. For her first three or four months Cathryn had reoccurring digestive problems. But I was blissfully unaware that Hal was concerned the radiation from my X-rays might have caused these problems.

Our pediatrician was a good friend of Hal's. They hunted together and often discussed our newborn daughter's health issues. The doctor's home was not far from ours and occasionally he dropped by to see Cathryn. I thought he must really like our adorable daughter and had no idea he was checking on her for the sake of my husband. I wasn't told this until years later.

After four months, Doctor Bill was sure she was completely healthy and promised Hal there were no lasting health issues to worry about. As for me, I'd always been convinced and knew in my heart she was in perfect health. Cathryn did have to wear a brace on her legs at night from the time she was six weeks old until eighteen months. Nevertheless, she was the happiest, most full-of-vim-and-vigor child I'd ever seen. There was no obstacle Cathryn couldn't overcome, and even to this day she is a strong, determined, and energetic young woman and nurturing mother to her own children.

EARMARKED FOR GOD

When Cathryn was eight years old, she was teased at school about the slight point on her ears. I told her it was the mark of God's hand on her ears, "God's earmark," as he'd been a shield to protect her in my womb. I told her her little ears pointed straight to Heaven and that she was part of God's wonderful and intricate handiwork. And definitely a part of God's plan and purpose for my life.

LEGAL EAGLE

Hal was engaged in his law career to expand and bring in new business. He was working long hours in order to make partner at his firm. Meanwhile, I was at home overwhelmed with motherhood, two young daughters both still in diapers, and I had no clue as to what I was doing. Until my marriage to Hal, I'd always had access to domestic help, but now by late afternoons I was still in my robe, with laundry up to the ceiling, dishes stacked in the kitchen sink, and both babies crying. I usually called over to Mother's, and Rosetta quickly arrived at our house to fix everything.

By the time Hal got home around 7 PM from work, dinner was ready to be served. After his usual scotch and water, he was ready to become 007. I was never really ready to be James Bond's girl, and I hated scotch! Every time I smelled it, I immediately retreated back in time to a dark and unwanted place. I began to feel trapped and hopeless. I'd not signed up for any of this, and my life was not working out like I thought it would. It was much tougher and harder work than I'd first imagined, and this was no "Superman" that I'd married.

LOOKING FOR A WAY OUT

One day, feeling hopeless and helpless about life's difficulties, I put the children down for their naps and went to Hal's closet and retrieved his twenty-gauge shotgun. Although failing on both previous attempts, this time I was going to make sure to end my life. I got the shotgun shell and put it into the chamber. The double-barreled shotgun was locked and loaded.

How in the world does one shoot herself with a shotgun? I simply couldn't hold it up to my head; it was too long. So I just sat there with that loaded shotgun, trying to figure out what to do. I glanced over at the dresser in our bedroom and saw my reflection in the mirror, which jolted me out of this trance-like morbid state. Then I heard one of our daughters crying from the other room.

"Oh, God, if there is a God, what am I doing?" I asked.

I fell on the floor and cried harder and louder to drown out our daughter's cries. Somehow I managed to get up and call Hal and ask him to come home. I simply couldn't take it anymore! Here was a struggling young attorney and his crazy wife was calling, demanding he come home or she will kill herself. It's hard to imagine what Hal must have thought and felt. Within minutes Hal was home. He put me and the two girls in the car, and we drove for miles with me crying in the front seat and two babies crying in the back. We stopped at a convenience store and got the girls a snack, and a pack of cigarettes and a Coke for me. Hal continued to drive until we were at least thirty to forty miles outside of Fort Worth, motoring toward and beyond Weatherford. By now our babies were asleep in the backseat, and I, too, had quit crying. It was time to head back home and get back on life's unfolding track.

Hal must have thought, *Who is this fruitcake I married?* But thankfully, he didn't say that, even though he had to have thought it at the time. He was completely committed to our marriage through better or worse—but he was sure ready for better!

CHAPTER 26

COFFEE HOUR CONVERSION

I thought everyone born in America was a Christian from birth,
sort of an American heritage, I guessed.

Two months later, a quiet desperation seized me to the edge of hopelessness and desperation once again, to the point where I wanted to give up. There were three choices: commit suicide, get a divorce, or stay. My pattern was that I always looked for the easy way out and, if possible, an immediate solution. Every day became harder and harder to get out of bed, so I began a survival routine from day to day.

Sometime in December of 1973, during this lifeless period, I was invited to a Christian coffee hour by Hal's sister, Shirley. Surely the invitation was supposed to read "Christmas," I was thinking. I didn't understand what a Christian was. I thought everyone born in America was a Christian from birth, sort of an American heritage, I guessed.

COFFEE HOUR

The coffee hour was held at Shirley's house, which was in a nearby neighborhood, so I felt obligated to go. I didn't know anyone there except for my sister-in-law and the person I'd gone with to the gathering. We were seated around the Christmas tree, and a young woman was introduced to give her testimony. It was embarrassing and uncomfortable for my friend and me. *How awkward and discomforting,* I thought, and I felt like leaving, but that would have been even more embarrassing and unacceptable, so I was stuck, and the lady I was riding with didn't want to leave.

So I listened to the woman's story. She was divorced, felt lost, and was unhappy. *Hey, sounds like me,* I thought. Then she did the strangest thing: she asked everyone to bow their heads and pray with her. Growing up, prayers were said by an Episcopal priest, not by real people. Nevertheless, I bowed my head and listened to her prayer. She asked who there might not have turned their life over to Christ, because she was going to say a prayer for them to follow. *I'd never tried this before, so what could it hurt?* And so I said the sinner's prayer and, unknowingly, received forgiveness and the gift of eternal life through God's Son.

After the party, my friend and I quickly fled. When we got to her car, she said, "Can you imagine anyone being so dumb as to say a prayer like that?"

"Who, me? No, I can't imagine."

And that was the end of that, I was a lot of things, but not dumb.

SALVATION REALIZATION

That was December 17, 1973, but it was not until February 19, 1974, at 3 AM one cold morning, that I finally understood what I'd done. While reading Hal Lindsey's *The Late Great Planet Earth*, I suddenly realized I'd already accepted God's gift of salvation through his Son. For the first time in twenty-four years of life, I instantly felt forgiven, loved, and accepted for being me, just as I was, warts, wrinkles, and all. This was my place of safety; this was my friend, the Light. I fell to my knees and wept with complete joy as the Light revealed Jesus Christ to me.

His presence was so real that I felt the glow of the warm love of God flood my body. It was like Jesus was stroking my head and assuring me I was loved and lovable! Immediately, I desired to serve and please God. The first thing that came to my mind was, *Get up and fix your husband breakfast. . . . You have got to be kidding, was my response to myself. "It's 4 AM!"*

By this time Hal and I had been married for a couple of years, but I had never cooked him breakfast. Each morning while I slept, he routinely and faithfully was up early, leaving at 7:30 AM for work to provide for his household.

I remembered that six weeks into our marriage, he had said one morning that his mother had gotten up every morning and fixed him breakfast while growing up. My smart-aleck reply was, "Great, stop by your mom's house. I'm sure she'd be thrilled to see you and fix your breakfast."

That was it as far as I was concerned, especially since I was still waiting in bed for my breakfast tray to be brought to *me*. That was what Rosetta had done for me every morning while I was growing up. She fed me and also took Mother her bed tray. Funny, both Hal and I were waiting for something that was never going to happen.

Now here I was, remembering all that after coming to the realization, after reading Hal Lindsey's book and sensing God's love at three in the morning, that God had revealed something to me that I could do for my husband to show him my love. So, at 4 AM on that cold winter's morning, I did get up and fix Hal's breakfast. Dutifully and willingly, while Hal was in the shower, I went to the kitchen, and when he came out of the bathroom, I stood there with a cup of hot coffee. He was quite surprised and pleased as I greeted him with a big smile. "You will never believe who was in our living room last night . . . Jesus Christ, and he is now in me."

CHANGED PERSON

Hal's mouth dropped, but he didn't say a word. After handing him the coffee, I said breakfast was waiting after he finished dressing. At that moment, Hal thought I'd lost it!

For the next two weeks, we didn't say a word about my coffee conversion. Frankly, Hal thought his fruitcake wife had finally flipped out. Before we married and while we were dating, the group he ran around with had told him I was emotionally unstable, and he was advised not to get involved with me. Fortunately, Hal saw potential in me, something no one else could see, a heart to care for and please him. He said years later that I was the first girl he'd ever felt really cared for *him*. And I really did, too! Hal had the love of a tender lamb's heart, too, under all his gruff lawyer exterior!

For the first time in the early years of our marriage, I became a genuine wife and housekeeper. No longer did I call for Mother's maids to come over to clean and do the laundry. I did these things myself, and amazingly, began to enjoy my new role. I had our girls bathed, dressed, and ready for bed by the time Hal returned home after work. A delicious meal was hot and ready to serve. I was learning to put him first in our marriage relationship, and he loved it!

WHOA NELLIE!

After putting the girls to bed, I would sit on the sofa while Hal read his newspaper. The Bible was now my new friend and comfort. I read the Gospel of John aloud. I thought it made as much sense to Hal as it did to me. After about two weeks, one night Hal put his paper down and looked at me. To me, it was a look of "Oh no, here it comes." He said I was gullible and would believe anything. As far as the Bible was concerned, it was not relevant for our times, and Jesus was a good man, but how could I possibly believe he was really the Son of God? Then he pointed to the front door and said, "You have one choice to make. You can go out on the front porch, but if you decide to come back in, that Jesus thing of yours stays outside."

I was shocked. We had never discussed God, and I had no idea Hal was so against him. That night I put my Bible in a shoebox and did not bring up the subject again.

LEGAL-SPEAK

Hal was just naturally domineering, and with the nine-year age difference between us, I believed he knew everything. He'd graduated in the top of his UT law school class, and I had very little college education. I was intimidated by his knowledge and intelligence. To make matters worse, he was an attorney and frustratingly logical about everything. He twisted my questions and answers to the point where I became confused about our conversations. These mental gymnastics usually ended up with me in tears, surrendering to his will.

PAYROLL AND SPENDING

From the time I was thirteen I'd received a monthly allowance from my Father's company. After marrying Hal, I worked part-time until our first child was born, but stayed on the payroll after her birth. My salary brought in additional income for us, which was good, but Hal didn't want my father giving me extra money for other expenditures and luxuries deemed necessary for my usual lifestyle. Father was chairman of a bank and automatically put money in my account each time I was overdrawn. I had an endless supply, or so I thought.

I overspent on clothes, jewelry, new carpets, clothes for the children; my list was endless. I didn't manage my finances properly, which finally resulted in Hal going to my father's office and telling Father that he—Hal—was now in charge of my money management issues. Father was not to give me any more money apart from my monthly salary.

This was an eye-opening experience for me. I was used to getting whatever I wanted, whenever I wanted it. Hal took away all my bank checks and credit cards and put me on a weekly cash allowance. When the cash ran out, that was it.

Little did he know that I'd memorized our credit card numbers. So one day, when I charged more than five hundred dollars at Neiman Marcus, to my utter embarrassment, the salesclerk returned with my ticket and announced that my husband was the only one authorized to sign on our account. Now, I was really mortified, and angry. *How could he do this to me?* But with my newfound faith in God, I did as the Good Book said: "Wives, be submissive to your husbands." Not only that, but another Scripture verse said that husbands might be won by a wife's quiet and gentle spirit, so I fussed and nagged less and began to love and accept Hal more, as imperfect as he was, to my way of thinking.

Tennis and Church

On Sundays, as Hal headed off to The Club to play tennis, I went to church with our girls. I was becoming active in the Episcopal Church, was on the Altar Guild, and attended a Tuesday women's program.

One Sunday in July of 1974, Hal surprised me and got dressed on Sunday morning for church. I could hardly believe it, and I was anxious to know why he had decided to go, but didn't ask. By this time part of my nightly routine was to get my shoebox down after Hal had gone to sleep and then read the Gospels and move on to other books of the Bible. I knelt beside my husband as he slept, and prayed for God to reveal himself to Hal.

Then one Thursday night in September while I bathed our two daughters, the phone rang. A few minutes later Hal came into the bathroom and told me his old childhood neighbor, Bobby, had called. He informed me that the next evening a young man from Campus Crusade was coming to visit us. On Tuesday mornings each week I'd been attending this women's Bible study at the church, where the wife of Hal's neighborhood friend led the group. She and her husband assumed Hal and I were on the same spiritual page. Hal left me and the girls in the bathroom to finish reading his newspaper. I fell on the floor and silently cried out: *Oh dear God, Hal has no idea this man is going to ask for support for his ministry!* I was a nervous wreck!

The Gospel

Within minutes after the young man with Campus Crusade arrived at our home, he could sense almost immediately that Hal did not share his biblical beliefs. So the young man switched gears and proceeded to pull out a copy of Campus Crusade's "Four Spiritual Laws." The pamphlet explains the Gospel in basic steps that lead to salvation. Hal held this pamphlet and followed as the young man read through it. On one page was a pictorial depiction of a chasm between two ledges. One side represented God, and on the other man, with the chasm separating them. The Campus Crusade man asked Hal, "How does God bridge the gap that separates man and God?" When Hal turned the page in the booklet, a horizontal crossbeam was placed on one side of the chasm, and there it showed how God has provided the way for man to cross over and be in a right relationship with God.

The young man looked at me and said, "Have you ever accepted Christ's payment for your sins so that you may receive salvation?"

"Yes, I did in December of 1973," I replied. He then looked at Hal and asked him the same question. Hal surprised me by saying, "I did about six months after my wife." He lied! But for the first time in Hal's life, at that instant, he understood the gospel message of salvation. At that moment he could no longer deny the truth of Jesus Christ, the God-man. After the man left, I showed John 3:16-17 to Hal. "For God so loved the world that he gave his one and only Son, that whoever believes in Him, shall not perish but have eternal life. For God did not send His Son into the world to condemn the world, but to save the world through Him" (*The Living Bible*).

SALVATION

On the following Sunday, September 28, 1974, my precious husband knelt in St. John's Episcopal Church and quietly surrendered his heart to Christ. His conversion was quiet, but Hal's tender heart was captured by God, and within a year he taught and testified with assurance the truth found in the Bible without any reservation or doubt. My faith was based on feelings and neediness, while his was based upon the authority of Scriptures and the conviction that God is who he said he is. I AM! What was true some two thousand years ago is still true to this day!

Carmyn age 3 in 1952

Carmyn at age 12 in Hawaii 1962

Carmyn 1967 Debutante

Rosetta and Carmyn 1995

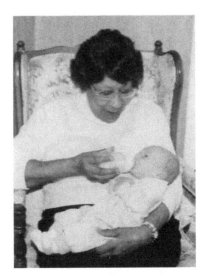

Rosetta nursing a third generation 2004

Carmyn's modeling portfolio 1970

CHAPTER 27

FATHER'S DEATH

*There wasn't anything I could think of to say to him to
bring peace to his heart and mind.*

On October 8, 1974, ten days after Hal's conversion, an event
happened that changed our lives in a dramatic way. My father
fulfilled a self-proclaimed prophecy. He'd spoken often about killing
himself and had always said there was a tree he'd chosen just across the
line into Erath County. That tree was the last thing he ever saw while
driving down to the ranch on that Tuesday morning. He was killed
instantly on impact, and the car was completely totaled.

ALCOHOL'S TOLL ON FATHER'S HEALTH

At age fifty-two, Father now drank morning, noon, and night. The
wrong choices he'd made his entire life were causing such an emotional toll on him and his body that the only pain relief he could find
was alcohol. Several times, while dining with Hal at the Petroleum

Club, Father had to be helped out of the dining room by the wait staff. Father's constant drinking, along with his anxiety medication and diabetes, began to drastically take a toll on his health, to such a degree as to be apparent to all.

Mother and Father separated and he moved to an apartment. He never returned home after that. He ended up in a one-bedroom apartment alone, with alcohol being his only companion. What a tragedy!

STALEMATE

During the aftermath of their separation, Mother continued to go through money like there was an ever-replenishing supply, while continuing to live luxuriously in their large home. Father's tiny apartment had none of the lifestyle luxuries he'd been accustomed to his entire life, so he began coming by our house at least twice a week to see me and his two granddaughters.

I shared with Father the newfound peace I had in God, but his lackluster response was that he'd read the Bible from Genesis to Revelation twice, and it was difficult for him to accept the simplicity of the Gospel. In Father's business-logic mind, he could not accept the foundational premise of God's love and forgiveness. All this God-talk was apparently just foolishness to him.

LABOR DAY

In September 1974, Hal and I held our annual dove hunt at the family Ranch. On Labor Day after our guests departed, my Father arrived. I remember that warm evening vividly as he sat with us on the breezeway overlooking the pool. We visited for at least an hour or more. The signs of Father's aging, worn-out body were plainly evident. He looked beaten down by life and his own destructive choices.

Three weeks later, on one of his visits to our home, he said he'd told God he was a complete failure and had failed at everything he had ever tried his whole life. There wasn't anything I could think of to say to bring peace to his heart and mind. I could only talk with him about God, but couldn't open his heart or mind to the truth of God's Word, and have him share in my new spiritual walk. I didn't know how to reconcile the past abuse issues between Father and me. For a brief moment, I felt guilty and blamed myself for the train wreck his life had become.

CHAPTER 28

A Lot of Ground to Cover

Father called . . . it was the last conversation I ever had with him.

Monday nights around 5:30 PM, Father usually called to talk. I knew he was lonely and lost, yet I didn't have the words to ease his pain. The Monday before he died, Father called at his usual time. I was on my way out the door with Hal and the girls. Actually, they were already waiting for me in the car, and I cut our conversation short. I told him I'd talk with him later in the week.

That was the last conversation I ever had with him.

I returned from Women's Day at the Church around 11:30 AM the next day. That Tuesday morning during communion, I'd knelt and prayed for my father. He was such a desperate, unhappy, tragic shell of a man, and I prayed for God to take him so he wouldn't suffer any more. After returning home, at noon I received a call from my brother, who was now managing the cattle herd at the Ranch.

"Dad has been killed in a car accident." Those words hit me like a concrete jack hammer. I fell to the floor screaming. This couldn't be true. How? Where? But it was true —all too true, and my brother filled in the details.

PROPHECY FULFILLED

My father had driven one of his company cars into a tree about a mile across the Erath County line, a few miles from the Ranch.

It was handed to me to give this news to my mother. She was not at home at the time; she was with the man twenty years her junior with whom she was having an affair. When I walked into the beauty salon where they were, she looked at my face, and hers turned pale white immediately. She knew what I was going to say before I even said a word.

Hal had driven me to the salon, so I could drive Mother in her car back to her house.

NEWSWORTHY

Father was well-known in business circles all over town, and news of the accident hit the local media outlets and radio stations. Visitors soon began arriving at Mother's house, but she stayed in her bedroom and called her hairdresser to come and do her hair at home. . I was in charge of greeting the many friends and business associates who had arrived to offer condolences.

A friend of mine took me over to a corner and, with a look of surprise on his face, asked, "Do you remember what you told me two weeks ago?"

"No," I answered.

"I asked about your new faith in God, and you said to me, 'God must know I am going to need him soon.'" He was stunned as he repeated this back to me. I nodded my head sadly, remembering, but little did I know how much I was going to need God, not only then, but in the years to come!

FINANCIAL CONCERNS

When Brother and his wife arrived, my first words to him were,

"Will I still be able to get paid my monthly salary from Father's company?" I had no idea what Brother knew about the business, but Father had been my financial security and I was terrified of losing it.

When Grandfather arrived at my parents' house, my father's accountant was also there. I told the two of them that I wanted an autopsy done. I wanted to know if Father had committed suicide. Grandfather grabbed my arm, looked at the accountant, and said, "No, let's get that coffin in the ground and the dirt on it as quickly as possible." He, too, was worried about money. The company's life insurance policy apparently paid only if Father's death was an accident, and then they would pay double indemnity.

FUNERAL

The funeral was arranged, and two days later Father was buried. Both of my grandparents blamed Mother for Father's death. Deep inside, I blamed myself.

CHAPTER 29

COME AWAY, COME AWAY

Aftermath . . .

After Father's death, Mother's ever-present drinking became even more excessive. And needless to say, Mother's relationship with me became increasingly hostile. Once again, she dreaded seeing me, and would say, "Well, here comes Miss Goodie Two-shoes with her black book."

DEPRESSION AND COUNSELING

Mother definitely did not like my newfound faith, and she continued to feel that she was being blamed for Father's death. She had no way of knowing that I blamed myself for his death. Father had died, and I never got to tell him that I forgave him. I never told him I longed for him to be my daddy. And I never told him how sorry I felt for him. I was never able to ask him what happened that caused him to continue to make wrong choices throughout his relatively brief life. Father went to his grave with my silence, and I was left behind with a myriad of unanswered questions, as well as the lingering guilt of blackmail. Those hidden secrets, ever-present in my mind, began to take their toll, and my relationship with Hal grew tumultuous. I withdrew my affection toward him and slid into another episode of depression.

It looked as if our marriage might be ending, but somehow I was able to convince him we needed marital counseling. He reluctantly agreed, but only if we went to Dallas where no one knew us. Hal did not want anyone to know we were getting marital counseling. So we drove to the Minirith and Meier Clinic. After a brief introduction and explanation of why we were there, the counselor began his background questioning. He asked Hal a few questions, then looked at me and said, "Tell me about your father. How did you two get along?"

Momentarily, I sat there in silence, and then suddenly the years of buried pain and anger could no longer be held back. I blurted out, "I hated my father!"

As our session came to an end, the counselor looked at Hal and said, "I don't think you need marital counseling, but your wife definitely needs individual counseling."

On our ride back home, I stared out the car window with tears streaming down my cheeks as I felt the smug presence of my husband. Of course he didn't need help, but I darn sure did! That was in May 1975, and I spent the next sixteen years going from counselor to counselor trying to find solutions and answers to fix myself. In reality, all I was doing was putting a bandage on a hemorrhaging emotional wound that needed more than a Band-Aid.

NEW ARRIVAL

January 23, 1976 brought a mix of joy and dread. I was carrying our third child and had gone into labor six weeks early. After twenty-two hours of labor, I was told that I needed to have a cesarean section. My other two deliveries had been fine, so why did I have to go under the surgeon's knife for this baby? I was terrified, particularly with the frightening prospect of being under an anesthetic once again.

Our third daughter, Allyson, was delivered while I was under anesthesia. She weighed five pounds and two ounces and was the most beautiful baby I'd ever seen! There were no marks on her face, and it was perfectly round and pink. Our pediatrician ordered her to be kept in an incubator for eight days. Each day she got better and stronger. She was a little bundle of joy, and that was something I desperately needed.

On the other hand, I was having a complete mental and physical breakdown following Allyson's premature birth. My obstetrician visited me on his daily rounds and said he was worried about me. After the delivery, while still in the recovery room, he said I'd grabbed him and kept shaking him, asking if I was dead.

There I was sitting in the private hospital room when I abruptly noticed I was holding two cigarettes, one in each hand. My body was shaking and my heart had been racing ever since the birth of Allyson. Now I felt like I was losing my mind as my past buried feelings were finally catching up with me, and in a very nerve-wracking, physical way. When the surgical nurses transported me into the operating room and put me on the cold steel operating table, I became terrified. I was deathly afraid that when I awoke from the nauseous gas that my baby would be gone. I cried and cried, but didn't know what to say or do about my apprehensions because I truly didn't understand myself what was happening.

After seeing me in this condition, the doctor decided to put me on Valium to calm my nerves. The Valium took me far, far away from my fears and pain. It would be several years before I finally returned to the reality of the present and learned to live without the sedative effect of tranquilizers.

Meanwhile, our marriage and my daily life suffered as I desperately tried to keep myself together mentally, emotionally, and physically.

CHAPTER 30

SENT AS A MESSENGER

Tears filled my eyes for the Grandfather I scarcely knew. But at least I had the joy of sharing God's mercy and grace with him . . .

Now that Father was gone, I seldom saw Mother. There were simply too many barriers and continuous verbal conflicts between us. Besides, I had my own difficult issues to deal with. I just didn't have enough room in my life to focus on repairing the relationship with Mother, and the recent painful events concerning both parents were too vivid and lasting. So I went in a different direction in an effort to get my own life back together.

At a cocktail party in December 1974, Mother had met a retired Air Force colonel, whom she called Pep. They married the following year, on December 24, 1975 in MacArthur, Texas. Once again, however, Mother was seldom sober. When she married, Hal and I were suspicious of Pep's motives, but it turned out that he was a true godsend for Mother and for us. Our family credits him with helping Mother stop drinking in 1979.

My paternal grandparents were now in their eighties and had begun calling me regularly to bring our children, their great-grandchildren, over to see them. I'd never had a close relationship with them, but still felt an obligation to be or become a part of their lives. They wanted nothing to do with Mother and still continued to blame her for Father's premature death. Following Father's death, Rosetta stopped working for Mother, so I asked her to work for my grandparents. She agreed and worked for them faithfully until their deaths.

Grandfather's Illness

In February 1981, seven years after Father had passed away, Grandfather had a stroke during an operation to clean out his carotid artery. He was in ICU for three weeks, and the doctors weren't sure how much longer he had to live; he had been completely unable to communicate in any form whatsoever. Visitation periods were allowed four times a day, for five minutes each. One day, when leaving a visit with Grandfather at the hospital, I suddenly felt a strong urge to return. The nurses were looking over his chart and changing his IV fluids. As I started to leave again, I was struck again by the inner prompting to stay, which was so overwhelming that I returned and went over to his bedside. As I picked up his hand, I gently said, "Grandfather, this is Carmyn. I want you to know that God loves and forgives you, and so do I. I am going to say a prayer for God's gift of salvation to be yours personally through his Son."

As I held his hand, I prayed the salvation prayer. "If you received this prayer, please squeeze my hand." His hand squeezed mine and he opened his eyes to look at me. Tears filled my eyes for the grandfather I barely knew. But now, at least, I had the joy of sharing God's mercy and grace with him, and hoped he'd received salvation.

The hospital staff moved Grandfather to a different room on another floor the next day. Although he could open his eyes, he never regained the ability to speak or communicate with me or anyone else.

Three times each week I went to the hospital and visited him. His eyes followed me, but that was the only response I ever saw. Once a week I took our three girls to the hospital to see him. They loved to take their art drawings, and our middle daughter, Cathryn, sat on his bed and read him her favorite story book, *Bears in the Night* by Stan Berenstain.

MY HOSPITALIZATION

During the first week of April 1981, I began running a body temperature of 103 degrees and was scheduled for a hysterectomy the following week. My GYN doctor lived only minutes from our house, and he stopped by on his way home from his office to check on me. He found me shaking uncontrollably and decided I should to go to the hospital emergency room. After several X-rays and blood tests, my temperature continued and would not break. Doctor Doug performed a laparoscopy to find out what was going on inside. His conclusion was that I needed the hysterectomy as soon as possible. Various medical tests showed that I had a cyst on one ovary and endometriosis on the other. A day later, I was sent home, still running a fever. Doctor Doug also concluded that I had a virus, and said it needed to run its course. So the plan was for me to return the following week for my scheduled surgery.

The next week I still felt terrible as the shakes and my fever continued. Since some healing time would be needed for me to recover from surgery, I realized my visits to the hospital to visit Grandfather would stop shortly. The day before my surgery, I went to the hospital and informed Grandfather of my upcoming surgery. As I sat on his hospital bed, I held his hand and told him not to worry about my whereabouts. I didn't want him to wonder where I had gone and reassured him that after healing from surgery, I planned to return and see him again, as before. I said a prayer with Grandfather, kissed his bald head, and left.

SURGERY; GRANDFATHER'S DEATH

That Wednesday morning at the hospital, I was scheduled for a vaginal hysterectomy, but as Doctor Doug began the surgical procedures, he felt resistance when trying to remove the uterus. He decided to make an incision to remove the diseased organs, and when Doctor Doug opened up my insides, he found that my appendix had burst and walled itself into the lining of the intestines. Worse, peritonitis had set in. Another twenty-four hours and I would have become septic and even more seriously ill. Following the completion of the surgical procedures, I was put on heavy antibiotics, and my primary care doctor was called in to monitor my recovery, along with Dr. Doug.

Once again, both during and following this surgery, the warm presence of my friend, "The Light," had manifested itself to me, and I experienced total peace as I was surrounded by its glowing presence. Two days later, following the surgery and while still in the hospital ICU unit heavily sedated, I suddenly awoke at 8 AM. There was then this same peaceful presence in the room, and I realized, "Grandfather has died."

Exactly one hour later, the phone rang and I was awakened again. The ICU recovery unit nurse handed me the phone. It was Grandfather's doctor and he said, "Carmyn, your grandfather passed away this morning."

While I felt sad that I couldn't make it to his funeral, even so I was grateful that by the goodness and mercy of God, I'd been able to tell him good-bye, that I forgave him, and loved him. I closed my eyes and thanked God for that precious opportunity, then drifted back to a restful sleep.

CHAPTER 31

THE GREAT DIVIDE

I was not going to embrace anymore false pretenses . . .

Recovering from my surgery, I was so glad be back at home since I'd been gone for eight days. But for some unknown reason, Hal seemed a bit distant, and intuitively, I knew he was holding something back. After a few days at home, reluctantly he told me that Grandfather's will had a handwritten codicil, and that he had changed his original will. I was surprised, to say the least, to find out Grandfather had left the bulk of his estate to Brother.

At first, I didn't believe it. How could this be true? Immediately I called Brother and said, "Please tell me that it isn't true. Why would Grandfather do that?' As I sobbed on the phone, Brother's rationalization was, "According to the Old Testament, it is the firstborn male heir that receives the inheritance of the family." That was his justification? I pointed out to him that he had two daughters and one son. Would he leave his daughters out? There was no hint of remorse from Brother as he answered, "No." Thus began a significant decline in our relationship. The disproportionate distribution of Grandfather's inheritance in Brother's favor was not only unjust but also totally unfair to me, his only granddaughter.

Ironically, however, the handwritten codicil was a bit vague and somewhat ambiguous. In order to forego a contested hearing, the probate judge required testimony from Big Red, Brother, and me for clarification. Thus, a negotiated resolution among all family members was necessary in order to reach an agreement regarding the correct interpretation of Grandfather's will.

COURT PROCEEDING

Two days before the scheduled Probate Court appearance, Big Red, now in poor health, showed up at my house wearing dark glasses. She rarely, if ever, came to see me on the southwest side of town at our home. The chauffeur had driven her over, and he brought in a large sterling silver butler's serving tray. She said she wanted me to have this memento because Father had bought it for her in 1943 when he traveled to England for the War Department. As quickly as her arrival had occurred, she departed. There was no wasting time and no false sentimentality from her, but for some reason unknown to me, it was apparently important for her to see that I received Father's gift to her.

The appointed day we were supposed to appear in court, I picked up the now frail Big Red and we met Hal at the Tarrant County Courthouse. Brother did not appear and had ceased all direct communication with me, electing to proceed only through our attorneys.

The estate attorney put Big Red on the witness stand and began to ask her questions about my Grandfather's will and the handwritten codicil. She was asked if there had always been this sort of overt male favoritism in our family. He repeatedly questioned her as to why their only granddaughter was cut out of her husband's will. Big Red was shaking and crying as she gave her quavering testimony, and the estate attorney had to help her back down and then escort Big Red to her seat. Next, I was called to the witness stand and questioned about the proposed compromise interpretation of Grandfather's will and codicil. Speaking from the bench, the probate judge made it known that the handwritten codicil was ambiguous and certainly not clear as to its proposed interpretation. If I agreed to the codicil's proposed interpretation, my daughters and I would be cut out of what the court felt we might otherwise be entitled to receive. That is to say, Grandfather's one-half share of the ranch would go to Brother.

Over and over, the Probate Judge questioned whether I understood what was taking place. He then told me to step down from the witness stand and motioned for Hal to approach the bench. They talked briefly and then His Honor, Hal, and the other estate attorneys went back into the judge's private chamber. Hal told the judge that I had agreed that the will should be interpreted as proposed. The judge obviously thought we were foolish, and made it clear to Hal that the court needed a signed document that would exonerate the court from any responsibility later on because of my perhaps questionable decision to surrender legal rights that otherwise might have been established in a contested hearing.

SETTLEMENT

Since I agreed not to contest the amended will, I insisted that distribution be made of my late father's corporation and downtown property, which he had left equally to Brother and me. Thus, by this negotiated quid pro quo agreement, Father's company holdings were divided and distributed equally between the two of us. That was the property exchange that prompted my agreeing to allow Brother to take the other one-half share of the Ranch property and cattle herd.

FRAIL RED'S COLLAPSE

After we left the courthouse, I took a frail Red directly to the hospital, her usual refuge of choice. The court proceeding had been too stressful for her, and she collapsed, emotionally and physically. Big Red could not hide the truth of the obvious male favoritism in our family. Finally, some of her established pattern of male favoritism was being brought to light. In her weakened state, she was never strong enough to get out of bed again.

About an hour after she was settled in her private room, Brother appeared with a bouquet of flowers. He tried to give me a hug and kiss, but I pushed him away. I was not going to accept any show of inclusion from him any more, nor accept the false pretenses about how much he said he loved me. I knew from actual facts and experience now that his pretended overtures were hollow, meaningless, and empty.

BETRAYAL

I felt betrayed by the one person in my family whom I'd naively thought could be trusted. I'd never disliked Brother in the thirty-two years of my young adult life, but on that cold November day in 1981, every ounce of perceived trust drained from my heart. Ten minutes later, he gave Big Red a kiss good-bye and again attempted to hug me, but I coldly refused his gesture. For the first time ever, I felt not only anger, but now a bitter dislike and distrust toward my former hero. We stared awkwardly at each other for a brief moment. Then he said, "I love you."

I didn't respond. It was a longstanding family greeting of hello and farewell to always say "I love ya," but at that moment I clearly understood his words were and had been empty and meaningless, just like our Mother's and Father's. I shook my head, closed my eyes, and turned away from him. Behind me, I heard the door open and close. Grieved by his behavior, I went to the window and stared blankly down into the parking lot below. After a few seconds, I saw Brother walking across to his car, and tears streamed down my face. My heart ached liked never before. The last hope of acceptance from my family of origin had evaporated before my eyes.

This bitter truth of family rejection became inescapably evident. Now I stood alone from my family of origin with the overwhelming reality that none of them appeared to love or truly care for me. Their actions spoke louder than their empty words!

CHAPTER 32

BURIED RAGE

It would be years before I understood the extent of her regret.

For two years after Grandfather's death, I arranged around-the-clock nurses for Big Red's healthcare at her home. It was a nightmare trying to keep the nurses happy, as each complained about the nursing routines and schedules of the others. I found myself spending more and more time each week at her house trying to keep everyone happy, and more importantly, attending properly to the needs of Big Red.

One nurse quit in frustration, but I soon found a replacement. Rosetta was there, cooking meals daily and planning soft diet menus. Willie D took care of the yard and minor maintenance around the house, while another maid took care of the household cleaning chores. Another lady worked as a secretary paying bills and taking care of the household expenses.

Brother and I were not talking, so we communicated through Big Red's secretary. His visits to Fort Worth were becoming less and less frequent, as he was busily absorbed in running the Ranch with an exotic cattlebreeding program.

HAUNTING MEMORIES

One day while I was at Big Red's home, she was startled when she awoke and saw me standing in front of her bed. She began to shake and cry as she said the devil had stood there and taunted her. According to her, he said she was going to burn in Hell for the things she had done. I hastened to reassure her of God's complete forgiveness. Even though Big Red watched Billy Graham's crusades on TV and received God's message of salvation, nevertheless, she was still afraid she couldn't be forgiven. Repeatedly, I explained to her that God does not judge sin on a curve, like schoolwork. Sin is sin to him, and it didn't matter whether we lied, cheated, or committed murder. It is all sin, no less and no greater. We all fall short of the perfect God's holy standard of righteousness.

One morning Big Red's favorite nurse called to tell me that Big Red wanted to see me. Within a half hour I arrived at her house. Big Red begged me to take her nurse to the bank and bring the contents of her safety deposit box to her. "I can't do that," I replied. "I don't have the power of attorney. Brother does. Besides, it's illegal for me to do that."

She looked at me with trembling lips and sobbed, "What I've done to you is wrong." It would be years later before I fully understood the extent of her regret.

NO PEACE

It didn't seem to matter how many times I would comfort and pray with Big Red, her fears and guilt over the past were firmly entrenched and buried too deeply. They had been held hidden from public view for far too long, and she never seemed to know peace during her lifetime. In retrospect, it was clear that she had conducted most of her life without regard for others or their feelings, nor for the consequences of her bad behavior. She had been content to skate on the surface of life and not invest with heartfelt care in family relationships. When push came to shove toward the end of her life, she was now terrified. Instinctively, she was increasingly aware that judgment was coming, and soon. Sadly, she didn't feel prepared, nor even forgivable or forgiven.

I'd made it clear to the home nurses that if Big Red got to an irreversible moment in her steadily declining health, she was not to be resuscitated. However, nurses are taught to save lives, and when Big Red quit breathing on December 10, 1983, the nurse automatically performed CPR until the paramedics arrived and transported her to the hospital emergency room.

The hospital called in the middle of the night and told me she had no brain waves and was technically dead (whatever that means). The hospital required a family member to sign the necessary release papers in order for them to remove the breathing ventilator. I was not about to perform that official act, especially since Brother had her power of attorney. So let him do it! I called Brother to tell him that this was going to be his job. But he was out deer hunting, and so it was left to me to attend to this final end-of-life responsibility for our grandmother.

Driving back to the hospital, I was furious. *Why me? Why are the family messes left for me to clean up?* This unanswerable question had plagued me my entire adult life.

Thankfully, when I got to the hospital, by God's grace, Big Red had already been pronounced dead, and I didn't have to sign any legal papers. Hal was with me, and the nurse took me into the room to identify Big Red. Upon seeing her lying on the gurney, I began to laugh and couldn't stop. It was so embarrassing. *What on earth did the nurses think?* I continued to laugh and finally realized that I was just inexplicably relieved that she was gone. Maybe now I could finally bury all the pain she evoked in my life. Little did I know that buried feelings never die, even when the perpetrator is dead, gone, and buried.

THE FUNERAL

The next days were horrendous. I took Big Red's clothes to the funeral home and arranged for the viewing of her body at the public visitation.

Our three daughters, now eleven, nine, and seven years old, accompanied me to the funeral home. They had never been close to Big

Red and, when in her presence, were naturally afraid of her. Big Red never had any nice things to say to them, as she mostly complained about everything from how the girls looked to how they talked and acted. They always fell short in her eyes. As did my husband and I; for whatever reason, we were never treated like extended family by her.

The funeral director took us to the room where Big Red's body was lying in the casket. He closed the door to give us privacy, and I went to the casket, stood there for a few minutes, and then touched her arm. It was cold and hard, and almost in a trance-like spell, I began to poke her arm harder and harder; years of anger, hate, and rage came forth pounding from within me. When Allyson, our youngest daughter, started to cry, I snapped out of it.

Then I bent down and took Allyson in my arms and said, "I'm sorry. I know you miss Big Red."

Through her tears Allyson said, "No, that's not it. I wanted to touch her too, and it scared me. She is hard."

Truer words were never spoken. She was as hard and cold in death as she had been in life. Once again I tried not to laugh. The woman lying in the casket was my grandmother and their great-grandmother. However, my daughters and I shed no tears for her. She was now a lifeless, cold shell, and none of us were up to pretending warm remembrances for the sake of appearances.

The funeral was uncomfortable for us all on both sides of the family. I hadn't seen Brother or his family for two years. Our girls had always been thrilled to play with their cousins when given the chance. Brother's youngest child asked our daughters who they were. When they said they were cousins, he replied, "My dad doesn't have a sister." That remark spoke volumes. He had told it like it really was; that was actually how his family felt regarding me and mine.

BIG RED'S ESTATE

Our family members gathered at Big Red's house after her funeral. It was déjà vu all over again. Big Red left her house and estate to Brother; her jewelry and personal belongings, china, and silver pieces, along with all the household contents, went to his wife. She left me a lump sum of money, which in comparison to her financial worth was relatively insignificant.

Several weeks later, Brother's wife called to tell me I could take my girls by Big Red's house and look through the remaining boxes before Goodwill picked them up. Once again, the familiar stab of family rejection was painfully thrust in my heart, and I felt devalued once more by my family of origin. On the bright side, however, our girls were delighted with all the shoes, hats, dresses, and purses that were left for them to choose from. Their precious hearts were not concerned at all that these items were the unwanted and undisposed leftovers of their great-grandmother. My daughters deserved more, but like me, they were not favored. While I didn't understand their reasons, my grandparents' hearts were cold and hardened to the fact that my children and I were also blood heirs. According to their relationship calculus, I and mine simply did not fit in as blood kin.

The truth was that none of my family's possessions and wealth could heal the longing in my soul of this yearning to be accepted by them. I so desperately desired to receive and hear those words of acceptance from my family of origin, but it was not to be. It seemed as though all that had happened recently with Big Red's death only served to add to my deep sense of low self-worth.

This painful seed of rejection by my grandparents had been deposited from the day I was born. On the day when Brother's wife called, that rejection drove me deeper into the black hole of shame and unworthiness that had permanently stained my self-respect. There was nothing, nor anyone, who could help me feel loved and approved by my family of origin. That relational pain held my heart hostage to the loss of belonging I had felt as a child. For the next eight years, I learned to fake it through my own brokenness over these family rejection issues.

MARRIAGE AFFECTED

My deep-seated emotions eventually became raw and exposed as I felt, once again, like an invisible child seeking to be heard and noticed. As the shadows of the past crossed my dreams again, nightmares woke me up and I couldn't get back to sleep because of the feelings and sensations I couldn't forget, memories I dared not share.

Sounds, smells, and touches to my body began to trigger all the years of secrecy, shame, and guilt, until finally I began to pull back from Hal physically. Every time we became intimate, the deep feelings of past sexual abuses and horror swept over me. Hal began to feel guilty for approaching me to meet his sexual needs. At the time he was in a men's Bible study group that met weekly, and one of the leaders in his group called one morning and asked if he could come by to see me. He wanted to talk with me about his concerns for Hal. Late that morning, he drove the twenty miles to our house and rang our doorbell. On opening the door, I wondered, *What in heaven's name is this about?*

I asked him to come in and offered a glass of tea, coffee, or water. He declined. We sat in the living room and immediately I felt very awkward in his presence. He began to read from I Corinthians 7:1-5. His interpretation of those verses were, it seemed to me, that a wife is never to refuse her husband's sexual needs, except for prayer and fasting. "Hal's needs are not being met, and you can have a husband who will be a grouch and angry, or an unfaithful husband. Which choice would you rather have?" His comparison stunned me.

I was flabbergasted, but what could I say? This man had a degree from Dallas Theological Seminary, so I took his words as gospel. When he left, I felt like a total failure as a wife. He had no idea of my past sexual abuse issues, but his words cut through my already fractured self-esteem. And so, I became the "Total Woman." In other words, biblically speaking it seemed, I was to lie down like a doormat and let my husband walk right over me. Memories of past sexual abuses were so graphic that I cried during our intimate times together as I assumed a man's needs were more important than for the woman. As I mentally relived my past emotional feelings of hurt, anger, disappointment, and betrayal, they were mingled with an even more painful yearning to be loved and cared for and not just an object of someone's pleasure. Mental and emotional confusion about my role as a wife according to Scripture distorted my perception of God. The "except for prayer and fasting" Scripture that Hal's friend quoted became a question I wrestled with at that time in my life. *What good did my prayers do? Does God even care for and hear me at all?*

As a child, night after night I had prayed and begged God to keep the Shadows away. No one told me, "This does not happen to you because you are a bad child." My entire view of sex was colored by maltreatment. Over the course of nine years, each time the Shadow entered my room, it felt like being raped again—just as the first time. I was not physically forced by the Shadow because I was afraid to try and resist. My submission to surrender again and again every time my free will was repeatedly violated by the Shadow's exploitation traumatized me—I was a victim of someone who displayed power and control over me. Even worse, this was someone I was dependent upon for my day-to-day existence. To be confronted once again with total submission and surrender, but now by a Christian leader who implied that I needed to put my physical and emotional needs aside, just did not make any sense to me.

The guilt, the secrecy, the creeping dread of lying in bed fearing, "Will the Shadows visit tonight?" all wore on me as a child. Now, as an adult, these buried feelings refused to die and go away. I became panic-stricken during intimate times with my husband by a certain way of being touched; the smells and sounds all triggered the past and reminded me of my abusers. I simply didn't know how to trust anyone, let alone God. Hal's friend's advice added fuel to the fire already burning within my soul. *There must be something wrong with me.* Thus, I concluded, *I am to be held responsible for either a frustrated or an adulterous man . . ?* This erroneous belief only further devastated my already fractured identity.

Incest was something I had never gotten over, even in our marriage relationship. The unlivable part for me was the continuing silence, the feelings I couldn't talk about. If this is such a vile thing that people can't even talk about it, then how vile must I be?

That frightening, scary little man with the huge hat that I'd hallucinated while under ether back in 1960 was right: "You'll never get out. You'll never get out."

Those deep-seated feelings of unworthiness, disgrace, and shame rapidly sucked me into the dark helplessness that seemed to surrender all hope for any end to the depressive spiral downward.

CHAPTER 33

DESERT STORM

I was waging my own combat . . .

On January 17, 1991, as America went to war in what became known as Desert Storm, I was waging my own combat in the desert as well. I was in Wickenburg, Arizona at The Meadows, an inpatient psychological treatment center. Ten days before the Gulf attack, I'd entered The Meadows for counseling in what had become a nightmare of continuous mental and emotional struggles over my past that were affecting the present.

My battles weren't directly in front of me, but due to the traumatic childhood, I was a prisoner of war in the present because of my past. From 1985 to 1991, I'd been hospitalized three times for clinical depression. At age forty-two, I'd been spending the majority of my days when at home, sleeping. I slept some days up to eighteen hours. Fortunately, I had full-time help at home. I could manage cooking and errands, but as to the rest of the housework, I was totally dependent upon the help. Even so, I managed to care for our three daughters, and they were my life's focus at the time.

Raising our three daughters had been a healing catharsis to my lost childhood, which was manifested through the many times of playing dolls, reading stories, trips to the park, and building Lego sets with them. All the things my Mother would not allow me to do, I made up for with our daughters. We had fun on Saturdays taking cans and boxes out of the pantry and then creating a makeshift grocery store in the playroom. During those years, I was more of a child than a mother, but those times are cherished memories for each of us now.

Following the birth of our last child in 1976, I'd struggled emotionally just to survive. Although acting normal, I was addicted to anti-anxiety drugs to keep me from falling apart. I was now on my fifth counselor. All previous counselors had been men, but I'd never felt comfortable sharing everything with them. There was one who told me not to be surprised if I fell in love with him during my recovery process. *What was that?*

PAST UNBURIED

By the spring of 1990 I was seeing a new counselor, a woman. A friend of mine from our church had led a women's Yokefellow group that I attended in 1982, and she suggested that I see this woman psychologist. (The Yokefellow group encouraged us to face our inner emotions and fears.) At these group meetings, I felt safe enough to share my buried feelings, especially with Linda, the woman who led our group. She was the first and only person I had ever disclosed the darkest secret of my childhood—rape—with. With keen insight, she realized as I shared this horrific truth with her that I was consciously unaware of what it meant for me to reveal this secret to her. She knew to wait for my abuse issues to surface again, when the right time and right place were safe. Then I would be able to acknowledge this bitter, repressed memory of those past abuses.

The only other time I'd attempted to share my sexual abuse issues was with a male counselor, and he had told me that I wanted to be sexually aroused as a child. So for years after that, I blamed myself and lived in a black tar of shame. Finally, with a female counselor, I felt safe and free to open up about my past, especially about the sexual abuse I'd endured. Anger, rage, and hurt poured from every cell in my body as I began to peel away the layers of the hidden darkness of shameful abuses from my past. I was becoming more aware that I faced an extremely difficult challenge, but had no idea of the physical pain and mental suffering my body previously had experienced in the past. I was totally unaware that the pain I'd gone thorough in childhood and adolescence was the driving force behind the devastating consequences that I presently endured on a daily basis.

FAITHFUL REMINDER

One night when awakened from sleep, Hal passed in front of our bed as he returned from the bathroom. Suddenly, I awoke and saw his shadow as he crossed the room. My heart felt like it stopped, and I couldn't seem to catch my breath. Intense feelings and remembrances of my childhood abuses flooded my mind and body. The familiar dark fear gripped my heart, and suddenly I felt small and powerless all over again. The Shadow seemed to have returned to my life again, threatening to take me captive to my past.

It got to the point where I couldn't sleep, so I sat in front of the fireplace and smoked cigarette after cigarette. Over and over I begged God to make the bad memories go away. During the day, I would walk on our six acres at the lake or sit on a retaining wall at the lakefront screaming as loud as I could, trying to rid myself of the demons of the past, which were manifesting themselves in the present.

On our property was an old guest quarters with an attached barn. One day I picked up the bat Brother had sent me, and I took framed photographs of Big Red, Grandfather, Brother, Father, and Mother along. After I placed the pictures in a row, I raised that bat and begin to scream, "I hate you! You ruined my life!" as I pounded and pulverized those framed pictures. Years and years of repressed anger, hate, and rage poured forth. The glass of the frames shattered as the edges of the frames were bent and crushed, and those pictures ripped apart as I continued smashing my tormentor reminders from the past.

Finally my hands and arms throbbed and hurt from the pounding jolts, and I fell on the ground and began to wail. Sobs that were so deep from within poured out, and my whole body shook.

I was tired, tired of pretending, tired of doing good, tired of detesting my life and hating myself. How could anyone love me? How could God love me?

At my wit's end, I found myself in the house, in the closet, curled up in a fetal position hitting my head against the wall. I just wanted to go to sleep and make it all go away. I didn't know which was worse, the pain from my head or this awful feeling of hopelessness, but I knew I couldn't survive another day in this deep hole of depression. For years and years I had tried to climb out, only to find myself sinking deeper in this miry pit. I was so, so tired of living in this dark place.

INPATIENT THERAPY

When Hal found me in this condition, he quickly called my counselor, and she told him I needed to be in an inpatient facility to deal with the issues of my traumatic childhood. At this point she was afraid I might become catatonic, and didn't want him to lose me mentally and emotionally. She said I had post-traumatic stress disorder and that I needed a safe place to go through therapy under professional supervision.

And so I left for The Meadows in Wickenberg, Arizona the day before our twentieth wedding anniversary. When Hal put me on an airplane to Phoenix, Arizona, I wasn't sure I'd ever come back. I feared I was just like my mother going away to mental facilities. The anxiety and fears of the sexual and emotional abuse I endured during childhood and adolescence had suddenly become too overwhelming for me to cope with any longer. Once again I was terrified and felt totally alone. Were my Father's words really true? Did mental illness run in Mother's family?

DETOX AT THE MEADOWS

I'd gone seventy-six hours without sleep when I entered The Meadows facility, and I'd been taking Librium, Valium, and Benadryl to try to sleep! My first stop was the detox ward. The patients there were a mess. We were from all over the country, and all of us were seeking to regain the desire to live again. We were all captives to dreadful memories of past abuses, appalling misconduct inflicted upon us by others, and painful thoughts about the past and the present.

The seven weeks I spent at The Meadows were the most eye-opening weeks of my life. I was there with others who had suffered other grievous injustices, abuse by perpetrators, and other physical and emotional trauma. There were soldiers recovering from the horrors of war, battered wives escaping the torment of beatings, rape victims, men facing their sexual addictions from past childhood abuse, and young boys and girls living lives of fear and dread from the atrocities of sexual, physical, and emotional abuse. We were quite a crew, all in the same leaky emotional boat. We were adrift and suffering from the continuous battering of waves that seemed unending. The extreme soul bashing that we all used to punish ourselves, with our negative beliefs, had been accepted as truths imparted to us by our oppressors.

Even though our stories were different, they were similar in terms of the devastating effect on our human dignity. We were bonded together by common feelings of fear, sadness, and loneliness. Pain and shame ravaged our bodies to their very cores. Our sense of self-worth had been blackened by the sins of the perverse madness of mankind. Each was trying to escape the degradation brought against us, along with the fear that we, too, could become like the perpetrators who had caused us to descend there in the first place.

This was life at its rawest for me. My heart, as well as my eyes, were opened to the extreme suffering of fellow human beings. We were all alike in this respect, and it hurt. In short, we felt hopeless and helpless in our individual sufferings.

UNFAIRNESS OF LIFE

While at The Meadows, I looked back at the past and tried to understand the "whys" of my life. For the first time I realized that life is not fair, at least not on the human level. One of the deepest core values of my inner self was fairness and justice, and here at The Meadows I realized how angry at God and life I was. What I wanted to know was, *"Why me?"*

As the days and weeks at The Meadows passed, I heard unimaginable stories from both men and women who eventually became like family. It was heartbreaking. The tales of abuse and the damaging consequences resulting from our collective pasts were unfolded and revealed to all in our group. Gradually, I began to have empathy and sympathy for the grief and suffering of others, and a new awareness about my own family abuse issues became clearer.

Abused people usually become abusive toward others. Now I saw my Brother in a new light, and I knew we had both done all we knew how just to survive. At this understanding I was finally able to release the anger and resentfulness I had held against him. I wanted to call and let him know, but so many years had gone by, and I was too afraid.

Understanding and Forgiving

Now, I wanted to ask for Brother's forgiveness. Previously, I'd always blamed our arguing over family finances on greed. This was because the only security our parents and grandparents had taught us was to put our trust in money. We both had just done what we'd been trained to do! It was all very simple, and yet, it was also a very profound new truth for me to face about myself.

The only difference in his life choices and mine was that I rebelled and used my sufferings to hurt others, especially those in my family. I'd been equally determined to make Father pay for what he had done, and so I used his wallet quite generously in order to receive a just reward for my silence.

On the other hand, Brother had been a dutiful and obedient son. From high school to college he'd played on the golf team and was an excellent golfer. Maybe, as had been his desire, he could have played golf at the professional level. Father and Grandfather were adamant about allowing nothing of the sort. Brother had given up his dreams for their demands. He must have felt like he had been the good son, while I was the prodigal and rebellious sister.

Tough Love

Perhaps the greatest piece of advice I ever received at The Meadows was a handwritten letter from a counselor. It said: "Carmyn, until you can see yourself swimming in the same sea of sin as your parents and grandparents, you will not recover from your emotional pain of the past."

Wow, did God offend my mind to reveal my heart's attitude. That was the hardest and most difficult truth I ever had to face about myself! I'd always promised myself that I wouldn't become like them, and actually believed I could never do anything like they'd done to me. Yet, when my oldest daughter was four years old, she said something flippant to me, and without thinking I turned around, and in slow motion, watched as my hand slapped her precious little face. Her beautiful, innocent blue eyes stared at me in shock. Innocence lost, just as had happened to me!

What had I just done? I began to cry and hold her close, telling her how sorry I was. But the damage had been done. I then closed myself off in a dark closet and said, "If there is a God in Heaven, please strike me dead if I ever raise my hand against one of my children again."

By God's grace and mercy, I never did physically abuse my children again. But now I understood that I was certainly capable of doing so. My Brother and I are living miracles to have gone through such violent and hurtful childhood experiences and yet not have continued those same patterns of abuse to which we were subjected.

Sense of Proportion Regained

How petty the family inheritance seemed to me now. Previously, I'd made money a god and had become like those I swore I'd never emulate.

True forgiveness, unconditional love, and compassion began to fill the many empty places in my heart. For the first time in my life, I realized it was not all about me. I now knew it never had been. Now that's true reality!

CHAPTER 34

RETURN TO REALITY

My uneasiness about the future was formidable . . .

When the day came for me to graduate from The Meadows, I was afraid to go home and face reality there. How would I do? Could I handle the pressures of everyday life? I'd been gone from my family for seven weeks . . . almost fifty days. Would our children accept me? The rules at The Meadows permitted one telephone call per week, and I had only visited with them by phone seven or eight times during my entire stay in Arizona. My uneasiness about the future was formidable, but I did realize it was time to go home.

Hal and our girls were waiting at the DFW Airport when I stepped off the plane. My heart was in my throat and my insides were shaking. Looking at my three little women, my daughters, I bit my lip to fight back the tears. But at the same time, I was so proud of them, as they had rallied together, running our home and keeping it in good order. They planned meals, did the shopping, kept the house clean (with the help of our maid), and continued to go to school, do homework, and attend their outside activities. My two oldest girls had planned and given a surprise birthday party for their youngest sister with cake, presents, and a few of her friends from the school. At that moment, I realized how blessed we all were as a family while we embraced at the airport.

EMPLOYING LIFE SKILLS

It took time for me to put into practice those proper life skills I'd learned while at the Meadows, including how to face life without pills. I continued to walk through my recovery process at home on a step-by-step basis. After I arrived home, Hal told my mother (still living at that time) and other members of the family that I'd call them when I felt like it. They were not to call me. Mother was furious, and on occasion she took her anger out on our daughters, especially my middle daughter, Cathryn.

One afternoon Elizabeth and Cathryn dropped by Mother's house for a visit. They both had their driver's licenses now, and a set of wheels. During their brief visit one afternoon, Mother went off on one of her vitriolic verbal rampages and spewed hateful words attacking Cathryn. Until then, our children hadn't yet seen this side of their grandmother. Cathryn left in tears, and for the first time they were both exposed to the biting force of Mother's cruel words. Now they could empathize with my hurts from the past that had arisen from her deliberately cruel remarks toward me.

Our children's compassion and newfound knowledge about my hurtful past helped them to then understand my struggles during their remaining growing-up years. For much of their childhood I'd been depressed, and they'd never fully understood why. A beautiful and wonderful healing process began to take place among my three girls and me. They realized for the first time what dreadful and traumatic events had molded my skewed beliefs and behavior in their lives.

As for Mother, it took seven months after returning home before I developed the courage to call and ask if I could come by and see her.

ENCOUNTER WITH MOTHER

I was so nervous while I drove to Mother's house that my legs shook. I dreaded this much anticipated encounter, but for the sake of my mental health I needed to confront her. After a brief and uncomfortable hello, Mother and I went to sit in her garden room. She glared at me. "So, I guess you blame me for everything?" *Here it comes,* I thought, but knew I had to state my case.

Trying to keep from crying, the words finally found their way out, and I was able to talk about those years of abuse I'd experienced. "Mother, all those years of Father's abuse, how could you not defend your only daughter? Surely you had to know what happened."

Mother stood up, yelled unspeakable words of condemnation at me, and then told me to leave. I did, but was glad to finally have that unhappy confrontation behind me. It felt good in an odd sort of way. I had taken a step forward to defend myself since no else in my family of origin had ever done so.

My relationship with Mother continued to be distant, cold, and hostile. Her words scraped scabs off the old wounds of harsh rejection and continued to feel hurtful in my heart. She said my aunts, my brother, and his family all thought I was crazy. She said they were afraid I was going to show up at their doors some day with a paper bag and then pull out a gun and shoot them. "People who hold this kind of blame do that," she snipped.

NOT WELCOME

Thereafter, my immediate family and I were no longer invited to family gatherings at my aunt's house for Christmas, or any other special occasions. When the girls were little, Mother's oldest sister would usually invite them two or three times a year to her house to join her for tea parties and other festive occasions. In the past, my aunt served the girls cookies and tea, and they adored her. They thought she was royalty because she was famous after having had a cookbook published. This aunt, who was well thought of and highly respected in her community, had always given each of them a present every year on their birthdays and at Christmas. But now, sadly, all of those invitations ended for my family.

I experienced new levels of rejection from all sides of my family of origin. Mother seemed delighted to inform me that the other family members had all gotten together on various occasions, but my family wasn't invited or included. She would also add, "I thought you were over all your hurt by now. Didn't they help you at The Meadows?" She said this sarcastically, to knowingly inflict the painful wounds of rejection by the wicked stabs of her hateful tongue.

Mother's bedside table had a framed photo of Brother with our cousin, my aunt's daughter. All the pictures of Brother and me that previously had been on her table were now gone. On the wall next to Mother's dressing table hung one photo of her, her two sisters, and Brother. Pictures of my family were no longer there. Mother continued to remind me again and again how much her sisters enjoyed Brother and his family, but thought my family members were religious fanatics, especially since my return from The Meadows.

My family of origin's rejection is never easy, but one would think that after so many years of experiencing this, it might have become easier. My mind said yes, but my heart still cried no. And so, I walled myself and our family off from the hurtful reminders of the painful past and the present.

But there was a new day coming, thank God, and of that I was certain.

CHAPTER 35

Encounter with the Telephone Pole

I know what I can do. I don't care what you think I can do!

In 1995 Hal and I were still struggling with our marital relationship. While I'd learned not to rely upon my past feelings, even so it was a constant battle to establish and create new thought patterns that were positive.

Whenever I visited Mother, she cleverly managed to bring down the wall of safety that I'd created for myself. Several times after I left her house, I pulled my car over to the side of the road and cried. My heart ached for her love and acceptance, but she continued with her barbed and critical comments. Why I continued to subject myself to this onslaught, I don't know. Perhaps I hoped that someday things between the two of us might change for the better. At least that was my hope.

Meanwhile, Hal was going through his own inner battles with his past. His family placed more importance on the matriarchal side of the family, and the paternal side was looked upon as the fifth wheel. In those days, Hal didn't feel accepted or approved, but ironically, his family didn't think he approved of or accepted them. Today, by God's grace, all his family issues have been successfully resolved.

IDAHO IMPACT

In March 1995 Hal decided that he wanted us to go to Boise, Idaho to attend an Impact Course held there. A counselor he was seeing had been through the course and suggested Hal attend for a life-changing experience. I was fine with Hal going, but he also wanted me to join him. Reluctantly, I agreed. After all, how many conferences, counselors, and self-help programs had I been to? Of what help would one more be?

There were five weekend sessions in the Impact course, mostly in Boise, each two weeks apart, and they took place over the course of three months. Each session lasted three to four days; we had absolutely no idea what we were getting ourselves into as we flew to Boise.

The first session was basic "Dr. Phil" 101. We each were individually confronted with our defining weaknesses and limiting qualities by the counselors and our fellow class members. There were fifty-four attendees in our group, and Hal teasingly called it the "Idaho 54th" after the movie *Glory*. That movie was about the first all-black Massachusetts 54th Regiment in the Civil War, under the command of Colonel Robert Shaw.

At Impact, together we comprised a ragtag group of different shapes, sizes, and ages from all walks of life. But we all had this common purpose of searching for meaning in life and, more importantly, for how to make life work. The games and life situations we participated in usually brought out our weaknesses, many of which we hadn't fully realized until then. It was hugely difficult, frustrating, and challenging. At times Hal and I both wanted to cry "uncle" and leave, but through the encouragement of others we hung in there.

THE ROPES COURSE

For the fourth bi-monthly session we flew to Salt Lake City, Utah to take part in what was called The Ropes Course. This was another significant turning point in my life. The ropes course was one of the most physically and mentally challenging endeavors I'd ever undertaken, and it included an attempted climb of a telephone pole. With heavy mountaineer boots on my feet, I was supposed to climb the thirty-foot-tall, eighteen-inch-diameter wooden pole. On the top of that pole was a 14-inch-by-14-inch platform, which I was supposed to pull myself up on, stand, and declare my affirmation statement—then jump for the golden rings suspended from ropes a few feet away.

For twenty grueling minutes I struggled, fought, climbed, and pulled my way up the pole. My arms and legs bled from being scraped over the splinters on the pole. Not accustomed to this grueling activity, I was physically exhausted, but kept on until I reached the top. With all my strength I tried and tried to pull myself up on top of that small platform, but it was no use. By now all of my upper body strength was spent. Fellow Impact members in my group below the pole cheered me on. "Come on, you can do it!"

I kept on struggling and pulling until, finally, it dawned on me. *How in the world do they know what I can or can't do?* With those words ringing in my head, I looked down at the clamoring group below, which included Hal, and yelled out a profanity and then said, "I know what I can do. I don't care what you think I can do."

The next question the group leader asked me was: "Then how are you going to get down?"

Thank goodness a safety harness with ropes attached was securely in place, and I was held in position astride that pole by a byline. So I let go and fell toward the ground as the safety line kept me from hitting the hard ground. The Impact group members, along with my husband, embraced my exhausted and thoroughly worn-out body. Everyone, including my husband, cried tears of victory. "You got it! You did it!"

THE IMPACT LESSON

That was the lesson! I'd finally learned to trust myself and my own good instincts. I had learned to say no to others . . . and I didn't need anyone else's approval or acceptance besides my own. I didn't have to prove to anyone that I was somebody that counts. *I am somebody,* and my feelings and life decisions are right for me, regardless of what anyone else may think or say. Unlike Father's fatal collision with a tree some twenty years before, the impact of this particular telephone pole had birthed in me a new life that actually indicated to me a hopeful future.

Returning from Salt Lake City, my sore body was bruised and blackened from head to toe. But now I was invigorated by a fresh new attitude toward life, and my dreams and hopes were not smashed. For the first time, it felt like I had personal power to be—and was meant to be—who I really am. Now I could stand up for myself with healthy self-regard, speak my mind, and set boundaries to keep others from using, abusing, or hurting me.

Shared Values

The Impact experience taught that I am a courageous, inspiring, and joyful woman of intrinsic self-worth. Hal and I developed a new respect for each other's individuality. We were learning to become a team without being codependent on or with each other.

The following January, 1996, we celebrated our silver wedding anniversary by renewing our marriage vows. And in 2013, we celebrated forty-two years of marriage together. We continue to grow in respect, appreciation, admiration, and unconditional love for one another.

CHAPTER 36

THE BIRD IN ICU

"Mother, do you think it was an angel?"

As a result of her years of smoking cigarettes and excessive alco-hol abuse, Mother went through radiation for throat cancer from 1989 to 1990. She had been an inveterate social smoker since age twelve, and now that she didn't drive, I drove her two or three times a week for her radiation treatments. During this time Pep worked Mon-day through Friday each week, and so I offered to take Mother to her appointments at the hospital. While she appreciated my taking her to her radiation treatments and doctor appointments each week, we con-tinued to be thorns in each other's side.

But now, to my surprise, Mother was actually a softer person to be around when she chose to rise to the occasion with her innate spar-kling personality. It had always been there, of course, just not with me. In her social persona, Mother never met a stranger and cheerfully conversed with all whom she came into contact with. By the end of their conversations, Mother knew the names of their children and other personal information, and she never forgot these personal details. Each time she saw that person again, she called them by name and asked how their spouse and children were. She made others feel important, and they seemed to love her wit and vibrant personality.

It would have been hard for most of her acquaintances and friends to imagine that she had a mean or vindictive streak. But I knew it was there on an experiential basis. Only those in our immediate family knew how often her cruel words and actions exposed her critical side toward certain members of her family, namely me and mine.

EMERGENCY SURGERY

The day after Halloween in 1996, I received a telephone call from Pep that morning. Mother had been taken to the hospital during the night. When I arrived at the hospital, she was having chest pains. Several tests were done, and finally, on the third day, she was diagnosed with having a tear in her esophagus. She was systemically weak, and her blood count was so low that the doctor said she might not survive the surgical repair.

On the fourth day of Mother's hospitalization, her two sisters, a cousin, and Brother gathered at the hospital to await the outcome of her surgery. My girls and I had not been around the rest of our extended family in years, and it was awkward for us to make small talk, especially since most of them appeared to be unaware of our presence as we were all together in the waiting room at the hospital.

POST-SURGERY

After four hours of surgery, the surgeon called us into a private room to discuss Mother's condition and the outcome. He said her stomach and esophagus had totally separated. He had done all he could do to stitch them back together, and now all we could do was wait.

No one said a word, so I spoke up and asked, "How did that happen?"

The surgeon explained that this was typical of people who threw up a lot. The room became silent, and no one asked another question. Mother was five-foot-nine and had always weighed around 100 pounds. I had long suspected she had an eating disorder, but now, at last, it was medically confirmed.

Mother's post-surgical condition continued to decline, and she was kept in ICU. She couldn't be removed from the breathing ventilator and thus was given a tracheotomy that replaced the breathing tube down her throat. She developed adult respiratory disease syndrome (ARDS), and the doctor emphasized that she had a long road ahead before being considered a survivor. I made the trip to the ICU ward twice a day to see her. Not once during my visits, extending over a period of weeks, was she able to open her eyes.

ROAD TO RECOVERY

The road to Mother's recovery dragged on for months, and this prolonged "recovery" period seemed to have no end. Naturally, I wondered if she would ever get out of ICU alive. Incredibly, she remained in ICU in a state of suspended animation for almost seven months. Then one day, quite surprisingly, she began to show marked improvement. Finally, she regained consciousness, and was moved from ICU to the recovery ward. There, attending doctors and nurses patiently helped to gradually wean Mother off of her breathing machine. It took another six weeks, but Mother slowly began to breathe on her own with the help of supplemental oxygen. She became fully awake again, but didn't seem pleased to see me on regular visits. The relationship barrier was still intact, in spite of her near-death experience.

On one occasion when I saw her, she said to go away because she was dying. By now Mother was deeply depressed, and it seemed to take the entire hospital staff to get her to go to rehab. However, in June 1997 Mother was released from the hospital, and a year later she was walking with a cane, completely off supplemental oxygen. Amazing what today's medicine and the human body can accomplish in terms of healing under dire circumstances.

MORE OF THE SAME

The ensuing years continued to meander by, and Mother's relationship with me continued to be hostile. When arriving for a visit, she would open the kitchen door next to the driveway and say, "You're not going to stay long, are you?"

One time I took my three-year-old grandson, David, with me. When Mother opened the door, David looked at her and said "Bye," and then he turned around and got back in the car. The simple words of a small child tell all!

Most visits to Mother's house were short. It was obvious she didn't enjoy my company, and her critical remarks were like a dripping faucet. Mother was always nitpicking, from how I wore my hair to why my children and grandchildren did this or that. I didn't look forward to seeing her, but faithfully held to the course I thought best. If she died suddenly or unexpectedly, I wanted to be sure she parted without any regrets from me.

ANGEL

About a year later I curiously asked Mother if she remembered anything from her time in the ICU. With a look of peace she then shared, "I was in a train or in a car and it was going very, very fast with everything whizzing by. There was no one driving, and I sat alone on the passenger side. But . . . " she continued, " . . . I wasn't afraid because a little birdie sat on my shoulder singing a beautiful song."

"Mother, do you think that was an angel?"

"Yes, it could have been," she replied.

CHAPTER 37

THE RELEASE

*Sometimes miracles seem to happen just by being
in the right place at the right time. . . .
Now I was being equipped to process thoughts and feelings
associated with bad memories, and this more or less instantly
changed the way I felt.*

In December 1999, Mother called and gave me the horrific news that my twenty-five-year-old niece had been raped. Working for the sports production department for a major television network, she lived in New York City and was walking back to her apartment late one evening after work. Someone came up behind her, put a gun to her back, and commanded her to follow him.

I couldn't listen to the details. My niece and I had not known each other during the period of estrangement from Brother and his family, but my heart ached and grieved for her pain and this traumatic infliction of harm in such a personal and degrading way. I wanted to see her or call and say something comforting, but it didn't seem like the time to try and reappear in her life. The ensuing months were very difficult and hard for Brother's family, and my heart cried out to them, but I remained silent due to the unresolved relationship issues that divided us.

MOTHER'S HEALTH ISSUES

By now Mother's health was starting to decline, and it was getting more difficult for her to walk without falling. Pep was also experiencing declining health with the onset of diabetes. Both were in their mid-seventies.

I found myself getting involved with health care assistance for both of them. Mother now depended on me to take her to doctors' appointments and to visit her older sister on the other side of town. Mother's other sister, who now lived in Central Texas about an hour and a half away, visited her sisters frequently. Since I was Mother's chauffeur, I was reticently included in lunch with the three sisters.

While these once-familiar relationships were still cold and distant, Mother's attitude toward me was slowly beginning to change for the better. Even though I was still experiencing difficulty with the rejection I'd felt from her and that side of the family, in a slow fashion things seemed to be improving somewhat. Even after years of counseling and self-examination, I was still dealing with some of the same inner self-loathing. Was this ever going to end? Once again I became depressed and was put back on antidepressants, but thankfully, to a lesser degree than before.

COUNSELING MIRACLE

Through teaching Bible studies at a nondenominational church, I was put in contact with a woman there who needed counseling. I recommended a counselor that I'd once used myself, but she refused to go because her ex-husband counseled with him. So I called around to find another counselor, and was given the name of Dr. Kembleton Wiggins, a Seventh-Day Adventist minister-psychologist. He conducted his counseling practice some twenty miles outside of town in Keene, Texas. Because it was not my custom to recommend someone I didn't know, I called and made an appointment for myself.

Sometimes miracles seem to happen just by being in the right place at the right time. Dr. Wiggins proved to be the exact right person! His counseling methods were unique and different from any others I'd seen employed. He did not believe it necessary to rehash the past or to relive previous painful experiences of abuse. This new "release method" was introduced to me, and it changed my life for good. Now navigating from the past into the present, I was at last headed in a new direction. Finally, I had discovered a new and energizing technique called "releasing" that successfully heals painful memories attached to the past.

RELEASING THE PAST

This new "releasing" technique involves becoming aware of what you automatically say to yourself in your mind; that is, how one's thoughts do affect feelings. In the here and now, these recurring feelings act to create emotionally driven behavior patterns, and often, negatively impact present-day actions. By releasing old thought patterns and systematically establishing new thoughts consistent with biblical truth, I began to understand "that was then (old past patterns), and this is now (new thought patterns)." My present-day thinking was being changed, and it began to make an incredible difference in my daily life. The wondrous moments of the present became my actual reality as I learned how to change prior false beliefs and thought patterns. With this new technique I was able to uncover and release subconscious misbeliefs, those that had previously held me hostage to the pain of my past.

With this life-changing method, I quickly began to experience a newfound joy with fewer setbacks. The added benefit was I learned how to recover more quickly from ingrained misbeliefs buried in my subconscious. Now I was being equipped to process thoughts and feelings associated with bad memories, and this more or less instantly changed the way I felt. It was so liberating, and now I was empowered to live according to the precepts and principles of the Scriptures, rather than what people said. This was truly life-changing, and I continue to use this method of releasing and canceling misbeliefs, to the extent needed, even now.

DEPRESSION LIFTS

One of the great discoveries made while being mentored by Dr. Wiggins was the statement that God does not violate human will. The choices we make and those others make may lead to grave consequences, but our free will is so important to God that he will not violate or impose upon our God-given gift of free choice. Former Arkansas Governor Mike Huckabee responded to Bill Maher's question regarding the wars, crime, and inhumane suffering in the world, summed up in the question: "How could God let this happen?" Huckabee's response was: "God does not rape another human being." Those are such powerful words, for God will not violate a person's free will.

All humans are responsible for their own choices. We tend to want to blame someone or something other than ourselves. But God should never be blamed for the evil and misery mankind has inflicted on this earth, or that which we suffer in our own personal lives. For years I'd been angry with God, blamed him for not intervening in my life when needed and for not getting me out of my painful experiences and hard circumstances. By releasing my anger toward God, along with releasing my blame and victim mentality, slowly I established a different perspective on life. My depression was noticeably lessening as I learned to put into daily practice this process of "releasing."

However, the most beautiful revelation of all came through my grandchildren. One night, during the wee hours of the morning, I had a vision of our family tree. It was in the envisioning of this family tree that I realized our six precious grandchildren would not be here had it not been for my life, or if I'd been successful at one of those suicide attempts. Tears rolled down my cheeks as I looked to Heaven and thanked God for my life. I told God I would go through everything again if it meant being where I stood at this moment in time. Things had indeed worked together for my good, and this good was beyond anything I could ever have imagined or dreamed possible.

Now I was in awe of Christ's words: "No love is greater than this, that a man lay down his life for another." I knew and experienced this greater love at that glorious moment and was at peace with all that had happened in my life, as it had all been worked out not only for my good, but for my family as well. Hope was reborn that night, and my faith in God had become fixed, firm, and unshakable.

CHAPTER 38

A Lone Pink Rose

*There on the birthday card was a photograph of one lone pink rose.
I was amazed and breathless.*

In June 2002, a precious gift reappeared in my life. The Yokefellow group leader, Linda, and I reconnected. It was a divine intersection.

Linda had earned a counseling degree by this time, and she asked me to attend a counseling conference with her at Wheaton College in Wheaton, Illinois. Happily, I went with anticipation of learning additional relationship problem-solving skills. I'd taught and shared, for many years, with women at our church on how to overcome painful issues of the past. Teaching was a favorite pastime for me; I was able to relate from personal experience with those who struggled with abuse or bad memory issues. I loved to teach and had many opportunities to individually meet with women suffering from these same types of childhood abuse issues.

Leanne Payne's book, *The Healing Presence*, was part of the curriculum for this conference. Ms. Payne also spoke at two or three of the teaching sessions, and for a full week I absorbed information on dealing with painful memories of the past. This conference turned out to be an invaluable learning experience, and I returned with great resources for helping other women with the abuse issues I'd experienced. As an added bonus, Linda and I spent hours each night sharing intimate moments from our respective pasts and baring our souls to one another. This was so important to me, especially since Linda was the first person to whom I unveiled the degrading incest of my past.

Our heart-to-heart talks throughout our Christian walk are treasured memories that have kept our friendship close. We don't get to spend much time together nowadays, but always pick up where we left off when we do see each other.

Someone once said: "There are friends for a reason, friends for a season, and friends for life." Linda is a friend for life.

THE ROSE APPEARS

The last day of the Wheaton conference was on my 53rd birthday. Ms. Payne was the speaker for the closing session, during which she asked us to close our eyes and ask God how He saw us. Immediately, a heap of ashes appeared in my mind. So I laughed to myself . . . that figures. But then I recalled Isaiah 61:3, where the Lord says, "He will give beauty and bouquets of roses instead of ashes." Then, instantly, out of the ashes, in my mind's eye, with my eyes still closed as the speaker asked us to do, a beautiful pink rose emerged in full bloom.

I was awestruck at this heartening revelation: *God sees me as a tender pink rose.* Tears filled my eyes as I realized this was my birthday, and my birth flower is a rose, a soft pink rose! Pink was the one color I'd always wanted to wear as a little girl, but I'd always been told it was for sissies. Joy and a sense of priceless value before God began to fill my previously dry heart, and I felt the warm sensation of an outpouring of God's love upon me. *God is my Heavenly Father; the Father I'd always longed to have. He will keep me in his tender and caring arms.* These words formed in my thoughts and were transforming my mind and restoring my soul.

I felt like Philip, one of Jesus' disciples, might have felt in the book of John, Chapter 14: "Philip said, 'Lord, show us the Father and that will be enough for us.' Jesus answered: 'Don't you know me, Philip, even after I have been among you such a long time? Anyone who has seen Me has seen the Father'" (John 14:8, 9). Slowly I knelt, and from the depths of my being, I thanked God for all he is, all he does, and all he continues to do. To then be awakened to experientially know God, not only as Savior, but also as my Father in Heaven, was undoubtedly one of the most spiritually transforming moments of my life.

BIRTHDAY CARD

The next day I returned to Fort Worth, and there were several birthday cards waiting for me on the kitchen table. Right away I noticed one in particular with its familiar handwriting on the envelope. Mother usually didn't send cards in the mail, but because I'd been out of town, this seemed the appropriate thing for her to do. I opened the envelope, and there on the card was a photograph of *one lone pink rose*. I was amazed and breathless!

My first inclination was to call Mother and tell her what had happened on the last day of the Wheaton conference. She gasped and told me she'd gone to pick out the birthday card for me herself. That was a miracle in itself. Mother always had the help do errands for her, but this time she actually went to the Hallmark store and chose this particular card for me. She said the card shop had an array of different types of flower cards, and there were several of colored roses. But she knew instantly the light pink rose card was the one she should get.

"Do you think that was God?" she softly asked.

Mother and I had rarely talked about God or spiritual matters after the death of my father. But one night during the Christmas holidays of 1974, I'd led Mother in a salvation prayer to receive the costly gift of God's Son. She had prayed with me, and said afterward, "I never knew before that I could do that." However, she was slightly under the influence at the time, and since then she'd not mentioned it again, so I'd wrongly assumed it was just a passing thing for her.

Here and now, Mother was asking if we'd just experienced a little miracle. I responded to her question, "Yes, Mother, I do believe with all my heart that is God's leading."

THE BLESSING

Even more precious than the birthday card was the blessing Mother wrote inside that card.

> *My precious Carmyn,*
>
> *My baby is growing up. And what a fine young woman you have become. I am so proud of you as a wife, mother, grandmother, and yes, as a daughter. I have learned so much from your gentle, kind way of life.*
>
> *Happy Birthday today—*
>
> *We always recited the following in the Episcopal Church, and Mother had added it to her words on the card:*
>
> *Many Happy Returns for the day of your birth—May sunshine and gladness be given—And may the dear Lord prepare you on earth for a beautiful birthday in Heaven."*
>
> *My prayers and all my love to you,* **Mother**

I hung up the phone, held the card against my heart, and quietly wept. I knew those words, written in Mother's hand, springing from her heart, I would treasure forever. One thing was for sure: miracles were beginning to happen all around me.

CHAPTER 39

MOTHER'S SECOND ROSE

In her golden years I was beginning to see a difference in her.

The new Mother opened up her heart to our relationship that had started to change after my return in 2002 from the Healing Presence Seminar at Wheaton College. She frequently began to invite me to visit her. Mother even asked me do errands for her, as well as take her to her many doctors' appointments. Amazingly, Mother welcomed me into her home and enjoyed being with her great-grandchildren, and I took them by often to visit her. She also loved my new companions, our two Bichon Frisè puppies. They are white bundles of pure love and happiness, and Mother laughed at their funny puppy antics. At least twice a week, and sometimes even three times a week, I made visits to see Mother. No longer was her usual greeting, "You're not going to stay long, are you?" Instead, she actually began to ask me if I would stay longer.

When Pep traveled out of town, I spent the night with Mother. She hated being by herself, especially during the night. These precious memories of being with her then are dear to me now. Although she'd never felt like a Mother to me in earlier years, now in her golden years I was beginning to see a different side of her. She had mellowed with age, and I beheld her now as a charming and witty dear friend.

NIECE'S UPCOMING WEDDING

In December 2002 Mother told me Brother's eldest daughter was engaged to a prominent newscaster in New York. They were planning a huge Texas-style wedding with all the preliminary events to entertain the many luminaries who were to arrive from New York.

Of course, Mother was anxious about her attire for the upcoming wedding, so I painstakingly scouted the department stores in Fort Worth and Dallas to find just the right outfit. By now Mother was confined to a wheelchair when she left home, so I made these shopping trips without her. I became Mother's personal wardrobe consultant, but after three weeks of taking an assortment of outfits back and forth to the stores, I was about to give up. Mother abhorred pastel colors, and the selection for a mid-morning wedding ensemble was limited. Not only was the color choice important to her, she also requested pants with a matching jacket, preferably in a light beige. This was becoming a task too difficult for me because Mother's taste was so exacting on what she wanted to wear that it was beginning to wear me out.

Finally I located the perfect outfit. With just three weeks before the announced wedding day, Mother was joyous over this selection. Her beautiful coral and diamond jewelry coordinated with the vibrant colors in the jacket, and the outfit looked stunning on Mother. It pleased me greatly that she was so thrilled over her attire for her granddaughter's wedding.

WEDDING PREPARATIONS

Since my family was not invited to the wedding, our plan was for me to help Mother get dressed and have her ready to be picked up to go to the scheduled wedding in downtown Fort Worth. The last time I'd seen my brother was at our aunt's funeral in December 2002. That day, as he was leaving our aunt's home, he made a point to call across the room and ask if I'd seen his daughter's engagement picture in the *Fort Worth Star-Telegram*. He seemed pleased that she was so stunningly beautiful; she is a silhouette at five-foot-eleven with dark hair and gorgeous hazel eyes. "Everyone says she looks like you when you were younger," he proudly beamed as he walked out the door.

My poor niece must have gotten tired of people telling her how much she resembled me. At times in her young adult life she would run into people who knew me at her age and was asked, "Are you Carmyn Sparks' daughter?" How I longed to have known her during the last twenty-eight years, but we'd only been around each other maybe a couple of dozen times, if that much! She is beautiful, talented, and a courageous young woman. And she and I shared more than our physical resemblance; we also had commonality in the horror of rape traumatically endured. Most assuredly, we might have related well and comforted one another, but the distance of familial separation over the years, combined with estranged feelings between Brother and me, were just too wide a chasm to bridge. However, I was thrilled that she was to be married in April and rejoiced vicariously through Mother's excitement and anticipation of the upcoming event.

Two days before the wedding, Mother called with the dispiriting news that the intended groom had backed out, and the wedding had been called off. I was shocked and my heart felt so heavy for my niece. Though I didn't know her well, my tears flowed freely for her pain. I couldn't imagine what ranges of emotion Brother's family members were experiencing. This event may have been a tipping point in Brother's heart for all the years of pain he'd locked inside. His daughter's horrendous rape—and now betrayal by the one she loved—must have crushed his father's heart. How I ached for him in the looming chasm of silence between us.

God knows how I longed to pick up the phone or drive to the small town where they lived and give them my consolation, but it was not my place. Time and distance had erected too many relational barriers between us. While my heart was broken for them, I lifted up many prayers on their behalf.

NEW DAY AND NEW CARD

April passed and then May, and I kept up with Brother's family through Mother on how they were doing. But not much information was forthcoming, and that was probably just as well for all concerned.

June 16, 2003 came, and I turned 54 years old. With this birthday came another card from Mother, with a brighter and deeper pink rose than the year before. It read:

> *Another Rose for my Rose—Sweet precious Carmyn, Oh how much I love you! I have so much fun with you and love our relationship. We have been through so much, but with God's strength and love, we have overcome. That is why we have such a special bond between us.*
>
> *Always stay as sweet and thoughtful as you are, and always remember how much your mother loves you.*
>
> *Also remember, "Never seek the wind in the field—it is useless to try and find what is gone."*
>
> *Happy Birthday and many, many more.*
>
> *The former Miss Bluebonnet—also known as Mother.*

In 1946 Mother had been chosen Miss Bluebonnet in a beauty pageant, and her photo appeared on the cover of *Southwestern Food Journal* that year.

I held the card with what must have been an expression of surprise on my face as I read her words. *Is this my Mother?* I thought to myself. Overwhelmed with bewilderment after I read her written words, I just stood there stunned at what I just read. I genuinely wanted to take these words to heart and believe them to be true, but only the passage of time would unfold the full implication of their true meaning.

I had no idea at that moment how significant this quote would become for me in the near future, but once again God was stirring the winds to shift and turn the tide inward. It would serve to breathe some harmony into the chasm of relational separation that had lain so long between Brother and me.

CHAPTER 40

A Hidden Pearl of Great Price

The years of silence had finally been broken.
What the enemy sought to destroy, God used to
produce a beautiful pearl of great price.

Thursday, July 9, less than a month after my birthday, the phone rang one evening around 9:45 PM. I couldn't imagine who was calling at this late hour. "Hello," I said as I picked up the receiver.

A voice from the distant past said: "Hey, Carmyn, it is Brother. Can you have breakfast with me in the morning?" *Was I dreaming?* After twenty-two years of not hearing from my brother, he wanted to have breakfast with me?

I could barely get my mouth open in time to reply: "Yes, I would love to meet you in the morning."

We set the time and place and hung up. I don't think I moved for twenty minutes. My mind and heart were trying to comprehend that, after twenty-two years of silence, he'd just called me. Next morning I was up early, dressed, and ready to go an hour before the appointed time. I was so excited and nervous that it seemed I could hardly breathe. Upon arrival at the café, he was already seated inside. I walked over to him and he actually stood up and gave me a hug. We held each other tightly. Brother and I were actually hugging after all these years of separation. The emotions of gratitude I felt were overwhelming and absolutely exhilarating. The years of silence had finally been broken.

CHILDHOOD RECOLLECTIONS

We sat down and I ordered some coffee. Within minutes, it seemed as though we'd never spent a day apart. Brother opened his heart and shared with me from the depths of his soul. Tears filled our eyes while I sat and listened for nearly two hours as he recounted our horrific childhood.

While at The Meadows, I'd been told that it's not unusual for two children who'd been through such traumatic events to break away in later years. The counselors at the Meadows called it "fracturing," where one child becomes the memory and the other needs to separate in order to survive. For years Brother had put me out of his mind. If I didn't exist, then his past didn't exist.

For the first time in my life, I was able to see and walk in my brother's shoes, and feel his pain and struggles. Some of the stories he shared with me about Mother and Father, I'd never heard. Several times when he'd come home from playing baseball, along with his friends, Mother was passed out, naked, lying on his bed. He was supremely embarrassed, and the other boys giggled awkwardly as they curiously looked at a naked woman. Ashamed, at age ten, Brother picked up our mother and carried her to the bedroom.

When he was just six, our Father had told him, "Son, I am leaving for good. It's up to you to take care of your mother and sister." My brother was bewildered as to what job he could find to feed us.

The almost unforgivable event he shared with me that day was the year he contracted strep throat, which advanced into rheumatic fever. He was hospitalized for several weeks. I totally recalled that on Sundays Father and Mother drove to Cook's Children's Hospital as I rode in the back seat of their Cadillac. They left me alone sitting in the car as they visited Brother. From the parking lot I could look up and see a window on the fourth floor and eventually Brother's face appeared. I jumped out of the car and waved and waved to him. Shockingly, on this our first visit in twenty-two years, I learned that Sunday was the only day of the week Mother and Father visited him in the hospital.

Story after story were recounted by Brother, and years of stored-up grief and sorrow flew from his heart to mine in that small breakfast café setting. I knew as I looked across the table that this was a man who'd been hurt by his parents, just as I had. It seemed to me Brother had reached out to me at this time in his life because his pain had become unbearable. It appeared he felt as if God was punishing him for his past. It was then that I reached across the table, held his hand in mine, and looked deep into his guilt-laden eyes. "There was nothing you could do to keep Father away from me, and there was absolutely nothing you could have done to help your own precious daughter when she was raped. You're not a failure as a father."

Compassion and loving-kindness flooded from my heart for Brother as I heard and felt his pain. Really, he was a living miracle. All those years he'd done the best he knew how to do, and neither of us had invoked violent abuse upon our children. The prior generation's sin patterns were being broken as Brother and I chose to live in more purposeful ways. That day, an empty place in my heart was healed; previously there had been only hurtful memories of shared abuses. And even though these were mostly painful memories of times gone by that we'd shared, his step to reach out to me after twenty-plus years of silence seemed to complete a chapter of my past with some sense of restoration.

PEARL OF GREAT PRICE

Natural pearls usually form when a parasite burrows through an oyster's shell and into the mantle tissue. The oyster's defensive reaction operates to surround the intruder with a membrane known as a pearl sac, and consequently, a pearl begins to form. This creative process aptly illustrates the childhood Bother and I endured. The intruders from the dark side of humanity had invaded and pierced our hearts. But what the enemy sought to destroy, God used to produce a beautiful pearl of great price. A pearl is my birthstone! Yes, miracles were showing up all around me, and this was truly one of the great redemption days of my life. Brother and I had opened that hard shell encasing our hearts and discovered a pearl of great beauty hidden within each of us.

We continued to visit regularly and to meet for lunch several times over the next several months. We would talk weekly, and the healing between our families became a source of mutual pleasure as we uncovered the genuine meaning of family.

VISIT WITH MOTHER

I told Brother that we needed to go over to Mother's house and let her see the two of us back together. But Brother said he wasn't ready. Oddly, Mother had always led me to believe the relationship she had with Brother was wonderful. I was surprised to learn from him it was only tolerable. From his ranching experience, Brother said that when a calf is born, the mother needs to bond with the newborn during the first hour or the calf will be rejected by the mama cow. "That is how it is with Mother and me," he said. Brother and I never knew a mother's nurturing care and love, so that bond between mother and child had never formed. How sad.

In September 2003 we met for lunch at a restaurant close to our Mother's house. Brother dreaded going over to visit Mother, but he was willing to do so for me. We drove over and stayed for about twenty minutes. The conversation was superficial, as always, and full of jokes and the teasing of one another by Brother and Mother. Surface talk, as always, was the only way Mother knew how to communicate with us.

Later that week, Mother told me she could die in peace now that she had seen her son and daughter reunited after years of separation. I laughed; it was always like Mother to try and find humor in everything. Little did I know how soon Mother would be leaving her earthly life.

CHAPTER 41

ROLE REVERSAL

Those were the first tears, and the only time I'd ever seen Mother cry.

In September 2003 Mother was basically limited to her wheelchair. That fall Pep became seriously ill with an infection that resulted in the amputation of part of his foot. He started therapy in a nearby rehab center. However, his diabetic condition worsened, and he was hospitalized again. The diabetes and high blood pressure made it difficult for the doctors to treat all the different symptoms he was experiencing. As Pep's health declined, I went to the hospital each morning to meet with his doctors, and then would leave the hospital, call Mother and give her a report. Later each morning, I'd pick Mother up around 11 AM and take her to visit Pep in the hospital.

Shortly after New Year's Day 2004, Pep's health worsened again, and now he was in critical condition. For three consecutive days I was called to the hospital for consults and updates on Pep's steadily declining health issues. It was exhausting, and I was just about spent from keeping up with Pep's health and making sure all concerned were informed on his prognosis. One morning as I drove across the freeway bridge on the way to the hospital, the sun was rising and glowed across my car windshield. It was beautiful, and I told God that I didn't think I could go on with this schedule much longer. At that precise moment this line from a song played on the radio: "He lifts me up to be more than I can be."

Nearing the End

Peace flooded my heart, and I knew God would give me the strength to go through whatever life placed before me.

On January 8, my thirty-second wedding anniversary with Hal, Pep was placed on a breathing machine and put in ICU at the hospital. It was now just a matter of time before he would be gone. Two days later I was called to the hospital three times in the early dawn hours. Pep had suffered cardiac arrest, but was resuscitated. I picked up Mother and took her to the hospital around 5:30 AM that last morning of Pep's life. She met with the cardiologist and internist and signed a medical directive DNR (do not resuscitate). Then I wheeled her into ICU to see Pep, and she held his hand one last time and said her good-byes.

Mother gave him a kiss on his hand, and told him how much she loved him. Tears fell gently down Mother's cheeks. Those were the first tears, and the only time I'd ever seen my Mother cry.

CHAPTER 42

MOTHER MELLOWS

*For the first time in my life, I felt like Mother actually
cared for me in a motherly way.*

After Pep's death, it became my role to take care of Mother. Her
only surviving sister wanted her to come live with her, but Mother didn't feel comfortable being that far from her doctors. Although
she wouldn't admit it, I think she wanted to remain close to me and
my family.

During the many car rides to the emergency room at the hospital,
and the long hours of tests and waiting for doctor reports, Mother and
I managed to talk about almost everything. However, Mother never
really opened up about her past. She'd learned to protect herself with
masks, and at age seventy-seven, it was just too painful for her to re-
visit the past and reveal the truth regarding shameful events she'd kept
in the back closet of her mind.

The only person Mother ever shared her past with was, oddly

enough, my oldest daughter, Elizabeth. When Elizabeth was sixteen, Mother told her she had been raped by her brother when she was twelve. Elizabeth, as an adolescent, had no idea what to do with such graphic information, and so she kept this information to herself until years later. It saddened me that my daughter had to be burdened with that awful family secret at such a young age.

Sudden Illness

On April 27, 2004, Hal and I were going out for dinner, but five minutes into our car ride, I told Hal to turn around and drive me home. I was sweating profusely and felt sick to my stomach. When we arrived home, I lay down on the bed and slept for two hours, but when I got up to go to the bathroom, I collapsed on the floor. My right side was paralyzed, and the pain in the right side of my stomach was so excruciating that I vomited.

My first thought was that I'd had a stroke. Hal quickly took me to the hospital emergency room, and I was kept in this hospital for four days. My blood count was elevated, and I had a fever that wouldn't go away. After numerous tests and an IV, I was released to go home with an unknown diagnosis. The doctors could only assume it was some sort of a virus that needed to run its course. That course, with bouts of intermittent fever, ran more than six weeks! It was exasperating and frustrating to us both for the doctors not to be able to diagnose the illness and, thus, they treated me symptomatically for fever and a nauseous stomach.

Mother became concerned and had her maid drive her to my house to check up on my recovery. She came twice a week to visit and bring food for Hal and me. She even called Rosetta to fix my favorite chicken and dumplings, but nothing seemed appetizing. I could tell Mother was really worried, and for the first time in my life, I felt like she actually cared for me in a motherly way.

Recovery

Gradually over a period of months, I started to get my energy back and was able to resume my daily routine and begin to "chauffeur" Mother again.

Now, with our newfound friendship, Mother wanted some colored jeans like the ones I was wearing. Since Mother needed a wheelchair to get around when she was out, it was difficult to take her shopping at the mall. However, since shopping was a priority for both of us, I used Mother's handicap parking sticker. We made a tour of ladies clothing boutiques. Mother stayed in the car while I went inside the store to put together outfits for her to make selections from. I then took the array of clothes to the car and showed Mother the choices available in her size.

MOTHER-DAUGHTER FUN TIMES

These shopping trips were some of the first mother-daughter things we enjoyed together. Finally we were able to enjoy each other and have fun together. I cherish these memories, because whatever we did and wherever we went, there was always plenty of laughing and good humor. Mother, along with Brother, are two people with incredibly sharp wits, and each also has a wonderful sense of humor. Even I was learning to be funny too! Life with my Mother was actually enlivening, even in her frail condition.

Mother and I were beginning to like, love, and enjoy each other, and it was truly delightful, even though a bit late in life arriving. A new dimension of pleasure in my life was unfolding, and I embraced it with all my heart.

CHAPTER 43

MOTHER'S DOWNTURN

*The cardiologist explained that a third of
her heart wasn't functioning.*

During the last two months of Mother's life, it seemed like I spent more time with her in the hospital emergency room than at her house. Since I'd become a certified hospice worker and volunteer, the training I learned from caring for the terminally ill was invaluable in caring for my mother.

Mother frequently called me to come over and sit with her. She actually seemed to enjoy having me with her at home. I lay across the foot of her bed, and we visited like two good friends talking about almost anything and everything, mostly lighthearted stuff.

During the mornings Mother had a wonderful caretaker, Alta, who cleaned house, did the laundry, prepared her food, and ran errands. Mother and Rosetta had reconnected by now, and occasionally Rosetta did some part-time work for her. At least three times a week Rosetta would receive a telephone call from Mother asking her to spend the night. Mother was always afraid to be by herself at night, and even more so after the loss of Pep.

THIS TIME IT'S REAL

On the afternoon of Monday, July 6, I received another of Mother's calls saying she didn't feel well, and could I please come and stay with her. At 6:00 PM she said if I didn't take her to the hospital, she would call for an ambulance herself. So this time it was actually serious.

The doctors admitted Mother to the hospital for further tests. Her blood oxygen level was very low, so they put her on oxygen and a monitor. When her oxygen levels dropped below eighty, the monitor beeped loudly and I prompted Mother—"Take a deep breath"—to help get them back up.

This went on for two days. Brother came to the hospital on Wednesday to relieve me and allow me some time to go home, shower, and change into fresh clothes. He faithfully watched the monitor and visited with Mother. She talked and joked with him the entire two hours he was there.

When I returned to the hospital and walked into Mother's room, Brother looked relieved. He told Mother good-bye and gave her a kiss on the cheek. I walked him to the elevator and he said that there wasn't any way Mother was going to die, that she'd probably outlive us all.

"She didn't quit talking the whole time I was there!" he said, rolling his eyes.

It was then I realized that it had been too long for my Brother to ever accept or receive love from our mother. In fifty-seven years they had never bonded; now it was too late for that to happen. As a child he'd shed many tears longing for a mother's care and love, but that desire had vanished long ago.

HEART PROBLEMS

The next day a cardiologist was called in to evaluate Mother, and he ordered a sonogram of her heart. As the male nurse pushed her down the hall, Mother asked him questions about his life. She had this incredible gift of making others feel good even in the face of her own difficult health issues. The male nurse left us in a holding room and said he'd be back after her tests.

The cardiologist arrived and wheeled Mother into the sonogram room. After a few minutes he came to the door and motioned for me to come with him. He took me into a room filled with medical equipment, and on the screen Mother's sonogram was displayed. It looked like a big blob, but I could see the heart moving. He explained that a third of her heart was not functioning due to damage caused by a prior undiagnosed heart attack. The tissue in that damaged part of the heart was inert, dead.

I was shocked. Mother had had a heart attack? When? He said it could have happened months ago; it was difficult to tell. He planned to meet with Mother and me the next morning to discuss her treatment options.

I returned to Mother and stood in silence next to her until the male nurse came to take us back to her room. When he arrived and said, "Let's go," Mother looked at me and said, "I am not ready for Greenwood yet." Greenwood is a local funeral home.

I spent three days and nights in the hospital room with her. Our precious daughter, Allyson, called and said she wanted to stay the night with Mother so I could go home and be with Hal. That night, she and our middle daughter, Cathryn, spent the night with their grandmother. All three of our daughters bless us with their selfless acts of kindness and their affections for me and their grandmother. They are truly a delight in my life, and I know they were in Mother's as well.

CHAPTER 44

MOTHER'S SAYONARA

Mother's humor never dimmed . . .
Today when I am at my wit's end about something,
I raise my hand and say "Sayonara!"
And sure enough, this too shall pass.

The next day following Mother's sonogram, the cardiologist came to her room and we talked about her next option. Her blood oxygen levels continued to be extremely low, and the doctor said the next step was to put her on a breathing machine.

After Pep died,. I'd taken Mother to see her attorney, and he'd drawn up a healthcare directive for her. Mother gave me a power of attorney to make the decision for her end-of-life healthcare treatment, if necessary. I never dreamed she would have presence of mind enough when the time came to make that choice on her own.

Facing the breathing machine issue proffered by the doctor, Mother looked at me and said, "I thought we agreed I wouldn't do that."

I asked the doctor to let us have some time alone to discuss her options. Mother and I talked about the options she faced, and she assured me that she just didn't want to be put on the breathing machine. The doctor was standing down the hall writing notes at the nurses' station, so I let him know Mother's wishes and asked, "How long do you think you can sustain her present condition?"

He said it was difficult to know. My mind was racing with questions. Should I call hospice? From my previous experiences with others going through life's end stages, Mother's physical condition was not yet close to the final stages of the dying process. I knew that most deaths follow a predicable course and felt we had at least seventy-two hours before Mother's body weakened to that point. It was Friday mid-afternoon, and so I decided to make those decisions on Monday. I was thinking to myself. *Let's just get through the next two days so we can talk this matter over with her family physician,* who was not on call over the weekend.

I went back into Mother's room and sat in the chair next to her bed. Each time the monitor beeped, I told her to take a deep breath. This went on for the next two hours, and Mother and I sat in silence with only the aggravating beeping noises of the machine.

MOTHER'S CHOICES

That afternoon Mother's eyes were closed most of the time, and she didn't seem to be awake. But she surprised me when, at exactly 3 PM, all of a sudden, she said, "Turn *Jeopardy* on. I want to see if that man keeps his winning streak." Her mind was keenly alert and aware of the time, and she wanted to watch her favorite afternoon game show. And by golly, she even answered some of the *Jeopardy* questions! Mother was still a master at trivia and crossword puzzles in the newspapers.

At 5 PM, the respiratory therapist came to Mother's room to give her a breathing treatment. Mother looked at him and said, "I don't know why they keep sending you in here. There is nothing you can do, but you can turn off that blasted machine." He laughed awkwardly, and I asked him if it was alright for me to leave and get a drink while he was with Mother. When I returned to the room he was sitting on Mother's bed, and they were engaged in deep conversation. He stood up and told me he had disconnected the monitor since there was no reason to keep track of her oxygen level.

He walked out of the room and then turned back around to say good-bye to us. Mother raised her hand and arched it across the air and said, "Sayonara." Her humor never dimmed.

The next morning the therapist came by to check on Mother. He said Mother had asked him what she physically could expect as the end drew near. He gently explained to her what she could expect. With tears in his eyes, he said, "I have never met anyone quite like your mother. She is a fearless woman, and I have deep respect for her. I just wanted you to know."

Today, when I am at my wit's end about something, I raise my hand and say "Sayonara!" And sure enough, this too shall pass.

CHAPTER 45

GIFT OF DYING WITH DIGNITY

Mother's gift: Going home gracefully
"I so enjoy you." With all our differences . . .
Mother appreciated me now
at the end of her life . . . joy and relief cascaded through
my soul . . . It was so heart-stirring. . .

About 5:30 PM on July 9, 2004, Mother motioned me to come sit next to her at her bedside. She smiled a beautiful smile and then said, "I am ready to go now; my little birdie is here." I assumed Mother was making reference to the same little birdie she saw in 1997 during her eight-month stay in ICU. Then she reached up, and with a gentle stroke of her hand, caressed the side of my face. And this was the backside of her dear little frail hand. Using the back of her hand was very significant to me. Previously, years ago, Mother's palm had administered slaps across my cheek, but now she chose to show forgiveness and healing by using the gentle backside of her hand.

Then, with her forever-memorable smile, she gazed into my eyes and spoke words I had longed to hear: "I so enjoy you." I always knew that, deep down inside, Mother must love me. I was her only daughter, and mothers can't help but innately feel love toward their own children. The joy of hearing my mother say she "enjoyed" me quenched the relational thirst I'd longed for these fifty-five years. With all our differences, inadequacies, failures, and flaws, Mother saw and appreciated me now at the end of her life. Not only that, but she also "liked" and enjoyed being in my presence. What warm feelings of joy and relief cascaded through my soul! It was so heart-stirring—then and to this day. I felt full-circle completion and closure with Mother, late though it was in arriving. The most important aspect to me was, and is, that it did happen, and I love Mother all the more to this day for her last gift to me.

Those four little words from Mother brought more healing to my heart than any she'd ever said. The lump in my throat was burning as I fought back tears. Not just "I love you," but more: "I *enjoy* you." She always told me she loved me, but those other words from her mouth had usually seemed so empty and meaningless. And now, *enjoy*? It was the richest blessing I could receive. I held her hand, stroked her forehead, kissed her face, and let her words soothe my mind and heart. Carefully, I lay next to her and hugged her the way I always wanted to be held. I prayed she felt the joy in my heart as I absorbed this sacred moment for several minutes.

Parting Gifts to All

Wiping away tears from my eyes, I gathered my thoughts and called our family together. Our two youngest daughters, Hal, my sister-in-law, and her daughters all came to say their good-byes. Mother smiled gently at each one and told each how much she loved them. Everyone tearfully said their good-byes, and Mother closed her eyes as she prepared for her journey through the valley of death. But she feared no evil, for she knew God was with her.

The nurses continued to come by and monitor vital signs. Each time I told them Mother was ready to die, and that those procedures were not really necessary. One nurse actually cried and said she'd never been with a dying person before. I was thankful for my hospice training having prepared me for something that is really not scary. The training taught me that Mother's care was in my hands and heart, not some high-tech medical equipment and instrumentation.

Hospice workers are taught to focus on controlling the symptoms of pain and discomfort, while doctors and nurses are trained to cure the disease. At the end of life, they don't really mesh. My work with hospice care had given me the privilege of being with patients during their last hours of life.

Naturally, as this was my own Mother, it was a good deal more emotional for me. But importantly, pain is not acceptable, or necessary, as I had learned. Pain relief medication can be administered in a pain-free way, but in such a way as to facilitate precious moments of tenderness and affection among family members. I was here to see that Mother made her journey of transition from life to death as comfortably and pain-free as possible.

AGITATION

Everything seemed to be going pretty smoothly, but at about 4 AM, July 10, Mother began to rail in the bed. It scared my daughters and sister-in-law. It looked like Mother was trying to get up out of the hospital bed, and I saw that her breathing was becoming shallow and labored. These were signs Mother was gasping for air. (It's an automatic response for the human body to fight for air, but thankfully, it is an autoimmune reflex that is not indicative of any cognitive feelings. Even so, it makes the attending family members uncomfortable and wanting to provide some form of relief to their loved one.)

Immediately, I went to the nurses' station and asked them to give Mother some morphine. They said a doctor's approval would be necessary.

"Then get a doctor's approval now," I said firmly.

Again, because of my work with hospice, I'd seen this occur many times before; I knew Mother needed some pain-relief medication right away to calm her agitation. Fifteen minutes later, a nurse came to the door and motioned for me to come into the hall. She told me morphine would suppress my mother's breathing. Of course, I realized that.

So I said, "Call the doctor and ask him." I was really exasperated by now with their slowness to appreciate the situation and to act affirmatively in giving pain relief. While I understood that most nurses and physicians are not trained to assist the patient in transitioning to death, even so, their jobs are to do whatever is necessary to calm the patient. I knew we needed for Mother to be in a hospice unit, but there was no time to move her now. Time was short, and Mother needed help to go through the dying process in a calm, quiet, and painless way. I was committed to do whatever it took to be sure my mother was as comfortable as possible. My hospice RN called us "midwives for the soul," as we are trained to help our patients labor through the dying process.

AT LAST, PAIN RELIEF

Thirty minutes later the nurse came in and gave Mother some morphine. During the next fifteen minutes her restlessness and agitation left, and she laid quietly. Mother didn't need to have another dose of pain medication, and for the next twelve hours her breathing was increasingly shallow.

By now, I'd been awake for almost sixty hours straight, and I was exhausted. My sister-in-law and daughter encouraged me to lie down and get some sleep. So I made the chair into a bed and slept. An hour later, our daughter Allyson tapped my shoulder and said, "She's gone."

TIME TO GO HOME

We hugged each other and cried. Everyone left, and I was in the room with Mother alone. I waited to make arrangements for her body to be sent to Greenwood Funeral Home. As I stood in the hospital room with Mother's lifeless body on the bed, I sobbed.

This deceased person before me had been my mother, but I'd never really known her as a mother. For whatever reasons, she'd been incapable of being a nurturing and a capable mother. This woman had given birth to me, and I am so thankful for my life. More importantly, I am thankful for the last three years with Mother, getting to know what an incredibly talented, gifted, and unique individual she really was. The last few years of life had mellowed her, and she was so delightful and fun to be around. Thankfully, I'd learned to enjoy her too!

She'd become a true friend in her later years, and now I knew I would truly miss her in the days to come.

DEATH WITH DIGNITY

Mother gave me the supreme gift of dying with dignity, and in return, I'd given her the gift of dying with respectful healthcare and comfort. I'd learned to be her caregiver as she labored in death and in transition from the natural into the spiritual.

Mother had told me to keep the beautiful outfit I purchased for her to wear at my niece's wedding when I offered to return it. Now I knew she was to wear this outfit as a symbol of another Wedding Banquet we will attend together in Heaven.

As I touched my Mother's cold hand, I knew God had always seen her capacity to be as she was at the end of her life. Miracles were manifesting all around, and those last years of Mother's life are how I remember her now. At her death, I was able to concur with God: "Better is the end of a thing than the beginning" (Ecclesiastes 7:8, KJV).

CHAPTER 46

MORNING SUNSHINE

All is well with my soul.

Mother's simple wooden casket was draped with roses of all colors. The hymn "Morning Has Broken" by Eleanor Farjeon was my request for one of the songs to be sung by a woman vocalist. I particularly selected this song because of my Mother's love of birds, and especially since God sent a precious birdie to escort Mother through death.

This song portrayed exactly what I felt. Mother's death became the new dawn and birth of my praise, appreciation, and thankfulness for her life. The Light had warmed Mother's heart toward me, her only daughter. And at the end of her life we were blessed with a new song in our hearts filled with affection for each other. Truly, God's mercies are new when morning has broken.

LIFE'S RETROSPECTIVE

I was to give the eulogy at Mother's funeral. Brother called and asked, "Will I recognize you are speaking about our mother?" I assured him, yes.

I am starkly honest about Mother, no holds barred. She never even fixed her children a peanut butter sandwich. There were no homemade cookies by her hand when we returned home from school. She didn't tuck us in bed or read bedtime stories. Basically, she'd been an absentee mother during our formative childhood years.

But now I focused on her last few years, and how remarkable she and Pep were. They had been such wonderful grandparents to our three girls. I shared memorable stories of the fun times they had with the grandchildren. Gratefully, Mother's grandchildren and great-grandchildren shed heartfelt tears of loss for their fun times together, and honored "Mimi"—the name they called her with their fond remembrances.

MAMA ROSE

While speaking at Mother's funeral, I saw precious Rosetta sitting with our family. She cried throughout the whole service. After the burial, when we returned to Mother's house, I found Rosetta sitting in a chair in Mother's bedroom. I walked over to her, gently kissed her on the cheek, and knelt beside her.

"Are you OK?" I asked with affection.

She slowly looked up at me with tears in her eyes. Then, affectionately, Rosetta gently placed her beautiful dark hands on my white face and said: "My baby, as I listened to you today, I thought, Who is that little girl? . . . my sweet baby, all grown up. She stands so strong, and I am so proud of her. I don't know how you did it, but you are . . . " and she couldn't finish her sentence. As I leaned into the familiar arms and bosom of Mama Rose, we hugged and wept together.

Leaning back, I looked into her beautiful brown eyes and said, "I do. Mama Rose, it was your prayers! You were always there for me, and Jesus, your friend, carried me and helped me to become strong for Mama Rose. God answered all the many prayers you prayed for me in ways we can't even comprehend. All is well!" (Those were the words to another hymn Rosetta used to sing during my growing-up years: "It Is Well with My Soul.") We held each other tightly, weeping bittersweet tears of joy and praise to God. Eleanor Roosevelt once wrote: "*Yester-day is history, tomorrow is a mystery, and today is a gift. That is why we call it the present.*" This was one of those sacred moments of the present, a timely and precious gift from God for both of us.

GOD'S HAND ALL ALONG

Once again, the breath of angel's wings passed gently alongside and caressed my face with the touch of God's hand. Now I could truly see that God has been with me all along and has carried me through my dark past. From the time I was almost three years old, when locked in my room as I nearly suffocated to death, God sent His Son in the form of a bright light. I believe Jesus cried, "If it be your will, let me take her now." In the silence of my soul's dark night, there came an unmistakable "no" from Heaven. Jesus wept, "Not my will, but thine be done," to his Father in Heaven. And then, Jesus strengthened my soul for what lay ahead and gave his angels charge over me to see me through the darkness of those things to come against me in the years ahead.

Gladly, though, God knows the end from the beginning, and he didn't want me to miss a day of all the joy that life holds. Now I knew it was God that had given me his grace to sustain me through my past, so I now trust that he will continue to grant me sufficient grace for the future. He has and does and will continue to fulfill his promise to be with me all the remaining days of my life.

Three days after Mother's funeral my oldest daughter, Elizabeth, who faithfully keeps a daily journal, came to me with eyes of amazement. "Did you realize you and Brother met exactly a year ago to the day, July 10, 2003? That is precisely the day Mimi died: July 10, 2004!"

"Is God sovereign?" was a question I never again needed to have answered.

Truly, his grace led me here. Yes, indeed, all is well with my soul!

CHAPTER 47

ROSETTA'S FINAL ROSE

"I thought you forgot about me."

A fter Mother's death, I continued to visit Rosetta regularly in her home in Fort Worth. She was in her late eighties now and only lived about ten minutes away. Our children and grandchildren frequently visited with Rosetta at her home as well. It was important to them to stay in touch with Rosetta as she was part of our family. On the holidays when my daughter Elizabeth came down from St. Louis, we would pick Rosetta up and spend the day together. Rosetta loved to say she'd taken care of three generations of our family.

Every other week, I went to see Rosetta at her home. She spoke of her friends in church, nieces and nephews, and those she'd faithfully worked for during her life. All of us made sure Rosetta was taken care of financially, physically, and prayer-wise. It was a privilege for us to arrange Rosetta's meals and healthcare during her later years. She was generally in a good mood, but sometimes complained about those who seemed to have forgotten about her.

ROSETTA'S NIECE

In October 2008 Rosetta continued to live alone at home, but beginning in 2008 her health began to decline. Her blood pressure was too high, and the medicine she took didn't always do the job. It became more apparent she no longer could care adequately for her own welfare. Her niece, Linda, recognizing Rosetta now needed full-time care, arranged to take her to live with their family in Kountze, Texas, which is a few miles north of Beaumont.

I spoke last with Rosetta before she left for Kountze in December 2009. She'd come back to Fort Worth to check on her house. This time when Rosetta called she was frantic. Said she didn't want to go back to her niece's place, but that she wanted to come back and live in her Fort Worth home. Although I understood that she didn't want to remain away from her home here, I also knew that being looked after by Linda was the best place for her. There she could be well attended to and cared for by Linda, since Rosetta really no longer had the strength or physical well-being to care for herself.

Before Linda drove Rosetta back to Kountze, I wasn't able to speak with her.

In January 2010, I called her former telephone number only to learn it was no longer in service. Naturally, I began to worry that something dreadful might have happened to Rosetta.

ROSETTA IN THE HOSPITAL

One day, fretting about Rosetta's whereabouts, out of desperation I called information for Beaumont. At that time, I didn't realize Linda lived outside of Beaumont, about 25 miles north in Kountze. The operator said there was no listed telephone number for a Rosetta Williams, and I was just about to hang up when she said, "But I do have a Rosetta Williams in Kountze." Thank the Lord for telephone operators who care. "Yes, give me that number, please," I quickly responded.

"God, please let this be her number," I prayed, dialing the number.

"Hello," an unfamiliar voice said from the other end.

"Is Rosetta there?"

"Rosetta's in the hospital," the woman said.

"Oh, what's wrong? Is she OK? This is Carmyn Sparks in Fort Worth," I anxiously inquired.

"Carmyn! This is Carmyn? Rosetta talks about you all the time!" I began to weep. "Where is she? I'll be there as soon as I can."

The sweet woman said her name was Guylene and that she lived with the Turners. She helped take care of Rosetta during the day while the Turners both worked. Guylene gave me Rosetta's number at the hospital in Beaumont.

Quickly I called the hospital number, and Linda answered the phone. We spoke briefly, and then she handed the phone to Rosetta. Rosetta began to cry. "Where are you?"

Then I told Rosetta I'd be there on Saturday. After we hung up I called our daughter, Cathryn, and asked her to drive with me to Beaumont.

On a sunny Saturday morning in March around nine o'clock, I picked up Cathryn and her daughter, Vayle, who was then fourteen. We made the seven-hour drive, checked in at the Grand Hotel, and received directions to St. Elizabeth's Hospital.

I held my breath when opening the door to Rosetta's hospital room. There was my sweet Rosetta! She had her wig on, blush on her cheeks, and pink lipstick. Blessedly anticipating our arrival, Rosetta had Linda help her prepare herself in this way. She was a welcome sight, but I was surprised by how much weight she'd lost since I'd last seen her. Her precious hands were curling inward as she appeared to be drawn up somewhat into a fetal-like position in her hospital bed.

When our eyes met, we both began to weep. I walked over to the bed and gently pulled her frail body into my arms and kissed her sweet face.

Between sobs, she said, "I thought you forgot about me."

"Never, Rosetta. How could I ever forget you? I'm here now."

CHAPTER 48

RECONNECTING WITH MAMA ROSE

As I held Rosetta, I recalled the times she'd held and comforted me.

In that Beaumont hospital, it seemed as though time stopped for a moment. As I held Rosetta, I recalled the times she'd held and comforted me. She began to whisper that she wanted to tell me something, and then Rosetta begged me to take her back to Fort Worth. She asked, "Where's Hal?" Rosetta wanted to see Hal, and I told her Hal would be coming down to see her soon.

For the next thirty minutes Rosetta tried to convince me that she needed to be back at home in Fort Worth. She murmured on and on about how she was left alone and mistreated. "I hear them talking about me, and they say I have Alzheimer's, but look at me? I know who you are, and I know where I am. Please help me." She kept picking at her ears, asking me to look inside. "All I know is I have fleas in my ear," she was saying.

Of course I knew she didn't, but then I remembered that when Rosetta was a little girl in Marshall, Texas, her mother and father hadn't wanted her. So they took her to an aunt, and the aunt didn't want her either, but reluctantly took her in anyway. Rosetta was told she was not part of her aunt's family, but since there was no other place to go, she could stay. Rosetta's room was on the old house's back porch, where she slept on a cot with the dogs. In earlier years she had told me one sad story after another of her loneliness and rejection back in the 1920s in those East Texas piney woods. And she emphatically recalled: "But those fleas sure liked me!" Rosetta had her own story of how she endured her own years of growing up with painful family rejection.

Now, at age ninety-three, in a Beaumont hospital, Rosetta still remembered those fleas bothering her from way back then, some eight decades before.

"Look who's here to see you, Rosetta," I said as Cathryn came near her bedside. Rosetta recognized Cathryn and was surprised at how much her daughter, Vayle, had grown. While they visited with Rosetta, I sat next to Rosetta's niece, Linda.

I reassured Linda that I knew Rosetta was being well cared for by her and her family. Rosetta's misery was based on not being at home in Fort Worth, and perhaps even more telling was her sense of loss in missing her friends back home. Even harder for her, of course, was not being totally self-reliant any more.

THE BOOK

After an hour or so, I told Rosetta we'd return in the morning. But before leaving, I showed her the new book manuscript I'd been writing about my life.

"This is my story about us," I whispered, showing her the picture of the two of us in my book. When Rosetta saw the picture of her at my wedding to Hal in 1971, she beamed and said: "You took me to Neiman Marcus to buy that outfit for me. You told me you wanted me to look special."

"Rosetta, you were always such a classy lady," I smiled at her, and then reminded her that I always thought she resembled the singer Ella Fitzgerald.

"When I return in the morning," I told her, "I'll read you some chapters."

Cathryn, Vayle, and I said our good-byes to Rosetta, and then Linda walked with us to the elevator. The three of us expressed our gratitude to Linda for taking care of Rosetta and ministering to all her health issues. In addition, I told her how grateful we were for her steadfast faithfulness to Rosetta in her declining years.

That evening, since this was our first time to visit Beaumont, we decided to visit the old, historic part of town and had dinner at the Spindletop Restaurant. The turn-of-the-twentieth-century pioneering discovery of the gigantic Spindletop oil well occurred in the early 1900s. It was one of Texas's earliest, and perhaps biggest, wildcat oil field breakthroughs, and the original well-site is situated just on the outskirts of the city of Beaumont.

With the advent of writing this book and reconnecting with Rosetta, it felt like I was reclaiming some of my own rich heritage with my surrogate mother. It had been a long road for us both to get this far in life, and that road had been fraught with perils, trials, and hardships. Although we'd traveled this road with different sets of eyes, our commonality in some of these difficulties had served to forge a bond between the two of us.

READING THE BOOK

The next day, when reading portions of my life story to Rosetta, we focused on the chapters about My Fairy Godmother and My First Rose. Linda and her husband, Nathan, and Saundra, another niece of Rosetta's, were also there to listen, and everyone seemed visibly touched as I related those chapters of my story that included Rosetta. Being so personal and open, we were all crying when I finished. Nathan stood in the corner of Rosetta's hospital room; he came over and said to me, "I don't cry," with tears in his eyes. Then he added, "But that is the sweetest story I ever heard. I had no idea you and Rosetta were so close. She's been calling your name out ever since she got here, and now I know who Carmyn is." We hugged and wept together.

This story of Rosetta and me came alive for me that day as well. Until then, I don't think I'd realized or appreciated what a huge influence she'd had on my life. But now, retracing that difficult past with Rosetta and family members, my feelings of sorrow were tender and exposed. I was emotionally drained and needed some rest. Cathryn, Vayle, and I headed back to Fort Worth after we left Rosetta in the hospital.

CHAPTER 49

SHEDDING SHAME

For years I had kept silent, but no more.

Cathryn, Vayle and I returned home on a Sunday with the following weekend being Easter. Two of our daughters, their husbands and five of our grandchildren gathered at our home to celebrate the occasion, and while they were there, Hal received a text message from my Brother: "Call me as soon as possible. We need to talk."

After everyone left, Hal called Brother, and his voice sounded agitated. He wanted to know if the family name was mentioned in my book. He told Hal everyone in his family was upset, and he was concerned that the family name might be ruined. He was so angry; I could hear his fretful voice through the phone.

Even though I wanted to talk with Brother to assure him that there was no mention of family names in my book, Hal thought it best not for me to do so.

Brother's wife came by our home late on a Friday afternoon; apparently my book was still a major concern. Hal and I assured her that there was no mention of the family name in the book. I chose to do this because it's my life story and certainly not meant to demean my brother or any of his family. It was then I truly realized how little Brother really knew about me, not to mention how little his family knew. Of course, I didn't go around calling Rosetta "Mama Rose" around our house when I was younger. But it was a special term of endearment for her that showed my feelings of affection and how deeply I felt about her; it was reserved mostly for the two of us. Hal, our children, and friends of Rosetta have heard me use that term for Rosetta for years.

After our brief visit, I walked Brother's wife to her car and hoped everything was all right between us. She assured me things would be OK and then left. That was the last time I ever saw or heard from her much to my sorrow.

In just a brief period, the newly reestablished relationship with Brother and his family had disappeared just as suddenly as it had begun only six years before when Brother called me to meet him for breakfast. The deep hurt in my heart concerning the silence between my family of origin was reopened. The relationships with my nieces, nephew, brother, and sister-in-law were broken once more. Once again I felt rejected by Brother and his family.

Wrestling with inner conflict, I considered giving this book up. My precious daughter Allyson asked me a great question one day when this was unfolding. Up to that point, I supposed, I'd never thought of it before. She said, "Mom, why is it that when someone exposes a crime about rape, society says, *Shame on the rapist*, but when someone exposes the crime of incest, society says, *Shame on YOU*?"

That question hit me right between the eyes. For years I'd kept silent, but no longer. I decided with boldness that I would never again let anyone pressure me to keep my life story in the darkness of inner shame.

The writer Montaigne says: "I speak truth; not so much as I would, but as much as I dare; and I dare a little more as I grow older." That expresses it quite accurately as the subject of truth-telling relates to me. Because I'd always lived in fear of betraying my family of origin,

I had withheld the truth of my tragic childhood and the abuse inflicted upon me for more than forty-two years. That fear enslaved me in bondage to the past, locked in a dark prison of self-hate. Now I dare to speak the truth, even though in so doing, it may cost the one thing I longed for my whole life—the love, acceptance, and approval of my family of origin.

Previously, my dark background had resulted in feeling unworthy of God's gifts and blessings. What the enemy intended for evil, God has redeemed and brought forth for his good in my life. Thus, I now dare to speak these truths with my whole heart, mind, and spirit. The person I became is due to the transforming hand of God. This is something only God can do. Because of God's love and work in my life, I have been transformed by tragedy. And not only me, but my own Mother also was wonderfully changed at the end of her life.

Since the disobedience described in Genesis 3, we are all marked with a virus, as it were, the virus of sin. The consequences of shame, secrets, lies, and betrayals continue to lie dormant beneath the masks of even the most respectable families. Sin separates us from God, but we do not have to stay separated and live a life of pretense. No longer do I have to pretend my past didn't happen in order to be safe. For years, wearing a mask and pretending had always been safer than being honest and open about my past. God provides the way for us, and his name is Jesus. Christ came to set the captives free, and I do choose to be set free—to live and walk in God's love. Alive now, I am living in the Light of truth, and to testify to what Jesus has done in my heart. When I was three years old God surrounded me in His light, and now I bear witness to the light.

LIFE STORY

This is my life story. Father violated my free will; Mother neglected me; Big Red abused and hurt me; both my grandparents rejected me as a person but used me as a commodity to enhance their own self-importance. My family of origin had been content to parade me around as a beauty object before their social peers, but it was all from their pride for "show and tell." My parents' and grandparents' hateful conduct against me in the dark—where their friends and the public eye couldn't see and know—was cruel, mean, hurtful, and unfair. And now I wasn't going to bury my grandparents' or parents' sinful conduct in the ashes and embers of the past. That kind of sordid and outrageous conduct can and should be revealed. I had come to the conclusion that it was time for their atrocious ways to see the light of day. I do not have, nor ever did have, the intent to ruin the family name. Their actions and choices to engage in their depravity bears their mark alone. How my parents and grandparents chose to live is more about their behavior and not mine or my Brother.

Why had Brother and his family come back into my life after twenty-two years of silence only to choose to distance themselves once again ? It is an open question that remains unanswered.

CHAPTER 50

THE HIDDEN THORN

Rosetta had something very important to tell us . . .

The week after Easter, Rosetta called from the hospital in Beaumont. She sounded anxious on the phone. She had something very important to tell us and wanted Hal, especially, to come with me right away. Two days later, Hal and I were on our way to Beaumont, and I asked Hal, "I wonder what's so important? Do you think she's ready to die?"

Hal laughed. "No, Rosetta is hoping I will help her fly the coop!"

We both knew Rosetta wanted desperately to come back to Fort Worth and be back in her own home. Even so, I still wondered what could be so urgent.

We arrived in Beaumont Friday evening, and I called the hospital to check in with Linda. She reported Rosetta was comfortable, but anxious to see us. I told her to let Rosetta know Hal and I would be there early the next morning. We invited Linda and her husband, Nathan, to come over to the hotel and join us for coffee that night. We discussed Rosetta's health and enjoyed getting to know each other better. They are a delightful couple, and we had a lot of family background information to exchange.

ROSETTA'S SECRET

After we had breakfast on Saturday, Hal and I drove over to the hospital to see Rosetta. She was happy to see us and, after exchanging a few pleasantries, she asked to speak to Hal alone. Ever since I'd married Hal, Rosetta loved him like he was her own son. She adored and respected Hal without reservation. When Hal and I had our troubles, I went straight to Rosetta and complained to her about him. She would look me straight in the eyes and point her finger right in my face. "You have a good husband; he loves you. Good husbands are hard to come by. You go straight home and treat that man with respect." I knew when Rosetta was finished on a particular subject, so I did just as she said.

Many times Hal called Rosetta and reported, "Carmyn needs one of your talks." No one knew me better than Rosetta, and Hal was quickly informed about my "tricks of the trade." But they both accepted, loved, and cherished me in a way I had never before been treated or loved, with the unconditional love these two continually demonstrated to me. How thankful I am for the spiritual examples of God's mercy and grace!

Linda and I left Rosetta's hospital room and went down to the cafeteria to have coffee. Linda was hopeful the doctor might be sending Rosetta home sometime early the following week. But there were many important healthcare arrangements to be made, and most importantly, Rosetta needed a sand bed to prevent recurring bed sores. Hal and I were glad to help out financially, and did so. Linda and her family, plus Guylene, were working literally around the clock to take care of Rosetta when at their home. Moreover, she wasn't ever left alone at the hospital, and they made sure all her physical needs were well taken care of in Kountze as well.

A short time later, we returned to Rosetta's room. Rosetta had told

Hal what she wanted to share with me and asked whether he thought I could handle this.

Hal thought it best for me to know, and said so to Rosetta. Everyone left the room so Rosetta and I could be alone together.

"Baby," she said as her eyes looked deep into mine, "the reason your grandparents treated you like they did is because they didn't believe you were your Father's child. They wouldn't accept you as their blood grandchild."

I couldn't believe what she'd just said! "*What?*" My mind was spinning, and it felt like I was gasping for air trying to understand what Rosetta had just said. Had she told me that my grandparents thought their son wasn't my father? I played that over in my mind—was I the product of a clandestine union between Mother and a certain former sweetheart in Mother's hometown? Mother had spoken of him often throughout my childhood. I even visited with him on most of our trips to her family's home when we stayed with her mother, my maternal grandmother.

This unexpected news sent me into a mental tailspin! Now I felt I needed to know if their suspicions were true. Thoughts and questions collided in my thinking. There were so many questions to be answered. Many of the missing pieces of the puzzle of my life, however, seemed like they were now beginning to come together in a clear picture for me. Did this explain the hate Big Red had for me all those years?

IN RETROSPECT

Rosetta continued on to explain to me that in September 1948, only a couple of years into their marriage, Mother had suddenly gone back to her hometown about four hours away. Apparently, she had decided to leave Father since she could no longer handle living with his parents. She was finally so emotionally broken with being subjected to the overt cruelty from, and continuing rivalry with, Big Red. Big Red's influence in her life was too overbearing, and Father was too weak and placating or simply unable to cut the relational umbilical cord with his mother. And that inexplicable inability acted as a corrosive toxin regarding his marital relationship with my Mother, and understandably so.

The biblical precept of leaving one's parents and cleaving to your mate had never registered with my father, or with Big Red for that matter. Giving them the benefit of the doubt, perhaps they had never heard of this concept, even though few sons, at age thirty, lived at home with his parents. Nevertheless, what Mother experienced at the hands of her mother-in-law was more than she was willing to continue to bear.

Irony of ironies, it was Big Red who went to Mother's hometown to retrieve Mother and bring her back to Fort Worth. During this excursion she'd found out Mother was currently seeing her old high school sweetheart, who by now was on his way to becoming a prominent leader in this town. Apparently, Big Red had caught Mother and him together in his car outside Mother's childhood home.

Shortly after this unfortunate occurrence, Mother discovered she was pregnant and truly didn't know who the father was. Since there was the distinct possibility that the baby she was carrying originated from Father, she knew there would be no way that he'd give up this child to her. And so, properly chastened, Mother returned to Fort Worth to have her baby.

Both grandparents and Father were predictably nervous and anxious at the hospital when I was born. However, upon looking at me with my dark skin, dark hair, and brown eyes, Father knew immediately I was his child. Thus, the name "Carmyn" was pronounced by Father for me, ostensibly after the Spanish gypsy in the opera *Carmen*. Father had told me all my life that he did not give me a middle name because he was adamant that I carry his name even after I married someday. No wonder he wanted to prove to all that I was his namesake!

There was never any doubt in Father's mind that I was his child. Especially since Mother's high school sweetheart had fair complexion with freckles, reddish blonde hair, and blue eyes. But even so, Father's parents were never able to accept me as their grandchild, especially since Brother and I had no resemblance to one another. Thus, from the outset of my birth, Big Red and my Grandfather questioned the identity of my birth father. As a consequence, I didn't qualify as blood kin to them. Not then and not later—in fact, never.

CHAPTER 51

THE TRUTH UNCOVERED

Light reveals truth.

Until Rosetta revealed this hidden secret, I'd been completely unaware of any misconceptions concerning my birth father. Now I wanted to clarify some of these issues from the past and confirm this past relational history of Mother as best I could some sixty years later. I was well aware of Mother's former high school sweetheart because we had met on several occasions when Rosetta drove Mother and me to her hometown for an extended stay. Desperate for answers, I called long distance information from my hotel room in Beaumont. Since Mother died at age seventy-seven, I quickly assessed that Mr. Barton was now in his mid-eighties. Hopefully, Mr. Barton (a pseudonym is being used here) was still living. As it turned out, his name was listed in the directory, and I was glad to get his phone number. The phone call was placed, the phone rang twice, and then a strong male voice answered. "Hello."

"Mr. Barton?"

"Yes."

"This is Carmyn Sparks, Mable Lea's daughter. Do you remember me?"

"Yes, Carmyn, how are you?"

"Well, I am in Beaumont, visiting Rosetta. Do you remember our maid, Rosetta?"

"Yes, I remember Rosetta."

"Is this a good time for you to talk?"

"Yes, my wife just left for church, and I decided to stay home today."

I held my breath. "I need to have something clarified that Rosetta just shared with me, and any truth you can shed on this matter will be greatly appreciated."

"Yes, if I can help in any way, I will try."

Tensely, I held my breath, and with a quivering voice said, "Recently, just yesterday, Rosetta told me that my grandparents, my Father's parents, never believed I was my Father's daughter." The words seemed to come easily out of my mouth, but inwardly I was on pins and needles.

There was a brief interlude of uncomfortable silence. "Hello?" Still more silence. *Oh great! I just gave this poor man a heart attack*, I thought.

Then, with the clearest and kindest voice, he said, "Carmyn, I am not your father, but I would love to have claimed you." I began to cry as I truly believed deep in my heart that I wanted to hear that Mr. Barton might be my father. Then Mr. Barton continued, and he told me that Mother was one of the kindest and sweetest women he'd ever known.

"Carmyn, this should have been resolved years ago," was his gentle reply, and I sensed warm empathy in his voice. By then I was sobbing almost uncontrollably as I uttered, "She stayed only because of me." Hence, this newly discovered truth opened my eyes to the unexplainable reason behind Mother's deep resentment toward me. Maybe if I had not been Father's daughter, she would have felt free to leave her caged and unhappy life with my father. Brother was, by then, already treated like Big Red's son, and thus, Mother felt little if any connection with Brother, who also felt no maternal bonding with her. For a glancing moment, I dared to dream and imagine that Mother's relationship with me might have been different if I had turned out to be Mr. Barton's child. But instead, I had become the continuous reminder of her lost chance to leave the prison of matriarchal control in our family.

I thanked Mr. Barton for shedding light on this dark secret that had been withheld from me these sixty-plus years. What a yoke of anguish was removed from my soul to know the truth about this hidden family secret.

THE LIGHT REVEALS TRUTH

While I wept tears of hurt, there were also tears of relief. Finally, I now understood why Big Red and my grandfather had disliked me so intensely. For some reason, that rejection now seemed easier to bear just by knowing they didn't think I was blood kin. So many pieces of the puzzle in my life were finally coming into focus to form a clearer picture. For instance, in earlier years, during the holiday season when our family photos were taken, Big Red would look at Mother and me and say, "Blood kin only."

Knowing how much Big Red and my grandfather hated Mother, I'd assumed their hatred toward me was because of that. And now it all made sense. It's strange how, sometimes, receiving clarity on a previously difficult issue can turn one's heart and soul lighter by just knowing the full truth.

Now also, I could finally understand why my grandparents cut me and my children down in their wills. Of course, Big Red's jewelry, personal belongings, family silver, china, and crystal wouldn't go to me or my children because my grandparents thought we were not blood heirs. Those beholden to live within the bloodline are held as the primary beneficiaries of family wealth. My grandparents had always perceived their name held prestige, status, and power. Their influence held my Father obligated to carry on this name for many generations to come. Now, for me and my immediate family, it was finally in the open: I, along with my husband and three daughters, was not and never had been considered family by my grandparents. No wonder my Father desired I carry the family name all my life in order to claim me as his daughter. For me this apparent revelation was like turning on a light switch, bringing clarity and understanding.

Light reveals truth. Certainly I could not agree with this warped and misdirected sense of family, but at least now I understood the why of so many things so much better.

My sister-in-law had told me that Big Red said she was leaving her personal effects to her. Apparently this was because, according to Big Red, I had told her, "I don't want anything of hers." However, in reality, I was never even given an option; that is, not until Big Red lay on her deathbed. The burgeoning guilt and conviction of knowing the wrongs she had committed her whole life fell open.

It was then I realized why Big Red had given me the beautiful silver butler's service that she brought to my house after Grandfather died. That silver service piece had been a gift to her from my Father during World War II. Maybe, I prayed, at the end of her life, she finally accepted the truth that her son was indeed my true father.

And she witnessed that, no matter what she'd said or done to me, or how badly she mistreated me, God had put it in my heart to serve her with kindness until the end. Sadly, Big Red never knew real peace in this lifetime here on earth.

CHAPTER 52

NO RESPONSE

Tears filled my eyes, and my heart felt torn.

It all made sense now, and I understood why I was never loved by our grandparents. Of course they loved Brother more and favored him. In their eyes, only he and his family were deserving of carrying the family name.

Although I had no answers for the mistreatment by my grandparents those many years, nevertheless I'd been able to forgive them years ago. They had acted as they did based on their misbeliefs. While this new knowledge didn't change my past or justify their actions, at least now I knew the ill-founded reason for their hatred.

Our parents, grandparents, and my story were certainly no reflection upon Brother or his children. The truth is, both of us had overcome great odds and become functional, nonabusing adults! We'd each chosen different paths to get there, with different lifestyles than our parents and grandparents. None of them were living any longer, and I'd waited to write my story until they were gone.

ROSETTA'S VIEW

As always, Rosetta was right in her earlier assessment. On my last visit, I'd told her Brother had demanded his family not to speak to mine. Her response: "Your brother and his family do not know you. The truth is sometimes difficult to bear."

Thankfully, my emotional pain and tears only lasted a night. By morning I was a renewed person. After all I'd been through with family-of-origin abuse issues, I wasn't about to let others hurt me again, at least not permanently.

THE PAST IN PERSPECTIVE

Once again, Brother seemed to fail to understand the reality of my dark and sordid past. When I was at The Meadows in 1991, a psychiatrist told me this frequently happens in families where childhood abuse exists. If one member of the family doesn't exist, then the reminders of the past don't exist. Some relatives will literally put another family member totally out of their mind in order to forget the past.

While my heart ached, I realized Brother does not choose to share his life with me. He's gifted in ranch management, with skills to care for the land he inherited, and his life seems complete without me. I can accept that, and I truly bless him with God's highest good. I have let Brother go with peace, forgiveness, and the prayer that his family blesses him with the unconditional love, respect, and admiration he deserves and needs.

Admittedly, however, I struggled with letting my sister-in-law and nieces' and nephews' families go. Two of their children had recently married and had just begun rearing their own children. I'd really enjoyed getting to know and be a part of their lives for a short while, especially since Brother's wife and I could share "grandmother" experiences. My two daughters who lived here locally really enjoyed connecting with their three cousins. Our family felt blessed to be able to share a part of their lives at showers and weddings. It took several months to get completely over the loss of those relationships.

KNOWING THE TRUTH

My friend Dr. Wiggins was a great source of comfort for God's healing during this time. He helped me to finally accept this situation when he wisely said, "Why do you want to be with those who do not choose to be with you?"

That truth was hard to swallow, but I finally accepted the fact that Brother and his family had chosen to discontinue any contact between our two families. It makes no sense when you think about it without blinders on, and now I could see this truth, even though it wasn't the picture I wanted to see. All communication completely stopped by Brother's family; it was if we never knew each other, much less that we were blood-related.

As much as it hurt to let Brother and his family go, I did so trusting and knowing that God's plans include his highest good for them as well as for us. And that doesn't mean we have to be or get together, or even be friends with each other.

The Bible comforted my soul as I read Proverbs 18:24, which tells us that "there is a friend who sticks closer than a brother." God has blessed my family and me with such caring and accepting friends—friends who will stick close, listen, care, and offer their support when it is needed.

CHAPTER 53

MEMORIAL DAY WEEKEND

We visited and talked about our lives together in earlier years. . . .
It was truly a memorable Memorial Day weekend for us all.

On the long Memorial Day weekend of 2010, Hal and I, with Cathryn, her husband and their three children, and Allyson, her husband, and their two children, all gathered together and caravanned in two cars down to Beaumont.

We went there to celebrate that festive weekend in Kountze with Rosetta and her niece's family. We arrived in Beaumont on Friday evening and stayed at the Grand Hotel. Saturday morning, we visited the early-twentieth-century McFadden-Ward House. About 1 PM, we headed back up to Kountze to spend Memorial Day at Rosetta's niece's house. The Turner family had planned a lavish spread of down-home cooked barbecue and good Cajun vittles for our eleven, plus another dozen or so in Linda's family.

Saturday morning was clear and bright with brilliant warm sunshine illuminating the Turners' tree-lined home nestled in the east Texas piney woods. Rosetta was thrilled to see us all together, and she thoroughly enjoyed being able to see the girls and our grandchildren. Even though she was confined to bed in the main house, everyone went in and out of her room for short visits. Children, black and white, were everywhere, ranging in age from two to eighteen. There must have been a couple dozen of us having fun and enjoying our families while we visited together that day. It meant so much for Rosetta and me to see my children and grandchildren playing and visiting with her nieces and nephews. We relished every minute of our time together, just being with and enjoying one another in such a peaceful and se-rene setting.

Linda and Nathan had said they were my family, and their expres-sions of familial love were heartfelt. We all basked in the warmth of their love and acceptance; it was like we'd known each other for years. I guess that's the way families are meant to be, without barriers of dis-cord and conflict. There's something really wonderful about engaging in friendly conversation over a sumptuous family meal at a holiday get-together.

GOOD VITTLES

We feasted on some real bayou country seafood, which included boiled crawfish, corn-on-the-cob, and barbecued ribs, all prepared by Linda's family. They were a joy to be with, and I marveled at the ease with which we all conversed and exchanged family stories. There's just something good and wholesome about family enjoying family, with-out reservation.

Most of the afternoon I spent sitting next to Rosetta's bed as she napped. When she was awake, we visited and talked about our lives together in earlier years. She cried, and I cried, but they were tears of joy for us both.

Every night since I'd given Rosetta a copy of the manuscript of this book, she would have Linda or Guylene read from it before going to sleep.

Rosetta said she hadn't realized how much I'd cared for and loved her all these years. And I learned that Rosetta felt guilty that she hadn't been able to do more to protect me as a child. I reassured her that she'd done and fulfilled all that God had sent her to do. She was a "for such a time as this" type of Esther from the Bible for me. In such a time as the late 1950s, there simply wasn't anything more she could have done to help me. Furthermore, as a practical matter, her being in a domestic caretaker role, she was simply powerless to shield me from harm.

Cathryn and Allyson thanked Rosetta for her enduring years of faithful service and loyalty, but more importantly, her genuine love and nurturing care. They asked her to imagine where I might be today if she hadn't been there for me when no one else was. She was truly a godsend in my life.

Hal sat and prayed with Rosetta, and comforted her, as she recalled story after story about the things she'd endured in her own childhood, as well as the family "secrets" regarding my parents and grandparents. She really had no choice other than to keep quiet about the wrongs she saw. Rosetta poured her heart out to Hal, and God used him to reassure her that she'd done her absolute best, and that was all anyone could do in her position. Hal's compassion and loving heart ministered healing to Rosetta's heart and soul. Those words of comfort seemed to bring settling rest to Rosetta's soul, and she was at peace.

Rosetta also had the joy that day to share with Hal that he was the answer to her many prayers for me as a child. He was kind, gentle, and protective, and she believed he was God's greatest blessing that God had bestowed upon me. She continued to tell Hal that he was what I had needed most in my unstable life, as he was strong with me when he needed to be. Yet, she knew Hal loved and adored me, and her heart was at peace knowing he'd always be there for me with his compassionate understanding.

Rosetta told me more than once, "They don't make men like Hal anymore. You've got a good man; be thankful." I wholeheartedly concur with her view of my husband.

TIME TO GO

Evening came, and it was time for us to leave. Our children and grandchildren had enjoyed the warmth of unconditional love and acceptance, as well as the joy of being with Rosetta's family. It was truly a memorable Memorial Day for us all.

My oldest grandson, David, turned sixteen that Saturday, and during our visit with the Turners and Rosetta, he came up and gave me a big hug. Then he said, "I wasn't going to come. Last night there was an end-of-the year school party that I didn't want to miss. But, thinking about it, I realized the party would last just a few hours. Now, I'm so glad I came and didn't miss this special day being with family." A true sense of family and loving each other is all I've ever yearned for. Now I have it, just not with some of those whom I'd previously thought mattered most.

At the end of the day my heart leaped with joy. All those "whys, ifs, and buts" held no grip or attachment on me now. This Memorial Day weekend was for me a capstone in my life, and one coming after years of wandering in the wilderness. The answer to the prevailing "why" questions in my life through the years was right before me in living color: my children and grandchildren. Now I know and appreciate that it's the mutual love of family members, each for the other, that endures and stands the test of time. Sometimes, as here, it turns out that extended family may be where true love is experienced and where warm acceptance lies.

Yes indeed, if all my questions about my name and who I am led me here, it's now that I truly know who I was born to be. And I do have that certainty of familial love that feels good and right. For me it springs from extended family, like Rosetta's.

Although I don't have all the answers, I do know that I'm finally free from the "whys" of my past. God revealed that all my questions had led me to this place of peace and acceptance, that I am who I was born to be, just to be in the here and now, and that truly, these are the sacred moments of life.

CHAPTER 54

LOVE'S ENDURING ROSE

My dark past . . . turns out to be the very place
God was cultivating fertile soil for a rose.

On February 23, 2005, at 4 AM, I wrote in my journal about Mother's death:

It has been seven months since my mother died. The reality is
that she is not on a trip, not away somewhere, but truly gone from
this earth, and it is now a certainty I cannot deny.

I will never hear my mother's voice again, never hug her frail
body, never touch her wrinkled little hands, smell her Quelques-
Fleurs perfumed hair and clothes, or see her feet in Isotoners shuf-
fling along with the help of her cane.

I miss her more than I'd ever imagined. Time's precious gift of
healing grief has brought the light of truth that no matter what my
Mother did in her life or with her life, and with all her mistakes,

her sins, and bad choices, she was still my mother.

It's a beautiful path of mourning, actually a surprisingly joyful journey of discovery. It's a pathway that is replete with the God of all comfort, which includes the peace of his Son, Jesus Christ. For in the here and now, his work of maturity demonstrates in the lives of his children that God is truly faithful and able to redeem all our hurts, all our pain, and truly bless us with his highest good in this lifetime.

Presently, it is simple to look back, and know and understand from this vantage point in time, why I alone couldn't fill the vast emptiness of my soul. That sacred pleasure is reserved for God alone.

While on the surface I'd known my Mother for fifty-five years . . . only during the last three of those years did I learn and get to practice what it was to forgive, accept, appreciate, enjoy, and truly love her, as God does in his forgiving eyes.

MOTHER'S PRICELESS BIRTHDAY CARD

In June 2003, Mother wrote a quote from an old Polish Proverb in the birthday card she gave me: "Never seek the wind in the field—it is useless to try and find what is gone."

These words illumine the truth that absolute forgiveness is possible only by giving up any hope of having a different past, while at the same time accepting the hurtful and wretched memories, and paradoxically, the joyful ones. To know God's love is all around me now, and in any given moment I may choose to love, be loved, and forgive and be forgiven, and this is all I need for the regrets of the past. The sacred moments of the present and the future hold endless opportunities for good. It is futile to seek meaning and purpose elsewhere, because these precious truths are found only in him.

THE WHY OF THE "Y"

My dark past, which previously I'd seen as one big heap of ashes, turns out to be the very place God was cultivating fertile soil for a rose. Yes, a rose with thorns, but now I can finally see where God has taken me in his hands, redeemed the years of suffering, and forgiven me for the many thorns I used to pierce others. But more importantly, he brought me to the place of forgiveness for myself, as well as for those who abused and hurt me.

God made known the treasures emanating from the darkness of my past and has given me abundant riches in those secret places of the soul. For now, I know it is God who calls me by name, Carmyn. If you drop the C and N from my name, it uncovers the "army" of a transformed child of God, protected by the angels that he gave charge over me. I have lived to find the "why" of the "Y" in my name! Thus, one simple pink rose arose from the ashes of the past, that I might know the truth of the present.

"I will give you the treasures of darkness and hidden riches of secret places, that you may know that it is I, the LORD, who call *you* by your name, am the God of Israel" (Isaiah 45:3, NKJV).

CHOICE OF REALITY: THE BLESSING OR THE CURSE

Then this stark reality hit me. My grandparents and parents went to their graves and, at the end, seemed like characters in a play that I'd never really known. Their lives were eventually concluded like the tragic finales of the operas my father repeatedly played in the music room as he drank alone. In Verdi's opera, Rigoletto's climactic third act ends as he cries out "The Curse!" and collapses.

God told the Israelites, "See, I am setting before you today a blessing and a curse: the blessing if you listen and a curse if you do not" (Deuteronomy 11:26, *The Living Bible*). I came into the realization that I'd chosen the blessing, but they had not.

By my choosing the blessing, the generational sins which had enslaved my parents and grandparents and held them in bondage were broken. Although they received God's grace before their deaths, they never experienced the abundant life in the land of the living.

I live to see and proclaim this goodness of God made manifest in the lives of my children and grandchildren. What a privilege, and for me, the ultimate blessing.

THE PAST REVEALS THE PRESENT

Yes, in a seeming paradox, the dark years of past hurts and abuses operated to nurture and nourish a tiny seed which, with the love of God in the redeeming light of his grace, combined to produce a song of joy. Because my name means "song of joy" and since God moved to put a tune in my heart, I am now who he created me to be. For now, my heart beats in rhythm with his, as I sing praises with a captivating melody of joy that is truly mine for the rest of my days. May the sweet rose of life in the present birthed in me become a fragrant aroma of his love for all whom my life may touch.

God does beautifully what we can only imagine. . . . He gives us more joy than we can ever dream, more blessings than our arms can embrace, and more love than our hearts could ever hold.

This is the story of one life, which, in God's hands, was transformed from ashes into the beauty of one simple rose. The Polish Proverb words shared by my Mother were right: yes, it is useless to seek the wind in the field. It is gone, but right here in the sacred moment of the present, it's a gentle breeze of miracles waiting to be walked out in our lives.

> *"What lies behind us and what lies before us*
> *are tiny matters compared to what lies within us."*
> —Ralph Waldo Emerson

CHAPTER 55

THE SWEET FRAGRANCE OF ROSETTA

*The sweet fragrance of Rosetta's life was because
of the sweet relationship she had with Christ.*

As I began my story with the passing of sweet Rosetta, so I shall end my story with her death. It was only after Rosetta's death that I began to understand and see more clearly the hand of God active throughout my life. It took looking backward to begin to see my purpose of going forward with all that God has taught me. As Romans 8:28 so beautifully puts it: "that in all things God works together with those who love Him to bring about what is good."

My life is truly a testimony, a witness to this Scripture. Only God could bring about good from the ashes of hurt, pain, and rejection of my past. God uses what is present in our lives to do the impossible. At the right time in my life, Rosetta was present to be used by God to show a deeply hurting and confused little girl what faith in God was all about, so that at the right times, and in the right places, God could reveal the love of Jesus to one of His love-starved little ones.

THE MEANING OF THE ROSE

The rose is a mystic symbol of the heart, and also of sacred and romantic love. Some believe that because of the rose's beauty and fragrance, it is a type of witness of the Lord Jesus Christ. Because of its abundance, and also because of the presence of thorns in the midst of the flower, Paul says in 2 Corinthians 2:14-16:

> *"But thanks be to God! For through what Christ has done, He has triumphed over us so that now wherever we go he uses us to tell others about the Lord and to spread the Gospel like a sweet perfume. As far as God is concerned there is a sweet, wholesome fragrance in our lives. It is the fragrance of Christ within us, an aroma to both the saved and the unsaved all around us. To those who are not being saved, we seem a fearful smell of death and doom, while to those who know Christ, we are a life-giving perfume." (The Living Bible)*

This beautiful metaphoric symbol, by which God teaches truth in the verses of this Scripture, is that of a fragrant perfume. Paul clearly implies in these verses that the Christian life, lived as it ought to be, is a pleasing aroma, not only to others, but to God also.

AS A WITNESS

The picture Paul uses illustrates to us that there is something about true spirituality when it is encountered that leaves a lasting impression. The Christian who has discovered this secret makes an enduring impact on those whom he or she encounters. This leaves behind an everlasting treasure of blessings, mysteriously present long after the last petal has fallen from the flower. The sweet fragrance of Rosetta's life was surely because of her sweet relationship with Christ, which was a witness to those whom she encountered. Surely I was and am a beneficiary of her sweet witness.

From the aroma of Christ in Rosetta's life, I was persuaded to embrace Christ in my life.

From my heart I have shared the good, the bad, the ugly. . . and the unimaginable. My desire is that my story may unfold like the petals of a beautiful rose—first as only a seed, then closed tightly in a bud, which amazingly begins to blossom as each petal unfolds. This process continues until, finally, a sweet fragrance comes forth by God's loving hand of grace and, with it, brings the joy of forgiveness and healing.

Ultimately, my prayer is that God might use the sweet aroma of his life in mine, to those saved and unsaved, to bring them to the transforming grace found only in him. For truly, with God all things are possible.

SOUTHWESTERN
FOODJOURNAL

A Regional Trade Paper — Serving All — Affiliated with No Groups

In Memory
Of
Mother
Miss Bluebonnet 1946

JUNE
1946
Volume 21   Number 6

Carmyn's Mother: Miss Bluebonnet 1946

Epilogue: In Memory
of My Mother

In 2006, I wrote the following poem, "One Simple Rose," as a tribute to honor the memory of my mother. My poem was selected for the Editor's Choice Award by The International Library for Poetry for best poem, and was published in 2007 by the International Library of Poetry in the volume *Forever Spoken*. This poem was the inspiration for my book.

One Simple Rose

Only piercing thorns between us,
Tragically love never grew.
Till one significant moment in June
Birthed a vision graceful and true,
Restoring beauty from the burnt ashes
Of trodden hope and abandoned care,
A stately pink rose miraculously appeared.
At last to mend the shattered brokenness
Of lament the hearts endured.
The gift of memories to so enjoy,
As a symbol of tenderness and
Fragrant sweet healing,
One simple rose eternally rests
Among the forgotten thorns.

Hal and Carmyn with their 6 grandchildren 2010

*"I remain confident of this: I will see the goodness of
the Lord in the land of the living."*
—Psalm 27:13 (NIV)

To God be the glory for all things he has done.

Printed in the USA
CPSIA information can be obtained
at www.ICGtesting.com
JSHW012022140824
68134JS00033B/2829